WIT
AND
WISDOM
IN
DYNAMIC
PSYCHOTHERAPY

COMMENTARY

"The keenest reading pleasure I know is that of coming across a treasured book read long enough ago as to be hazy in one's memory, thumbing through it and finding the choice passages underlined, and then reading them with that mixture of almost-for-the-first-time and the delicious faint echo of being reminded. Imagine, if you will, such precious tidbits picked from all the very best work in our field, past and present, from Freud to Kohut and Winnicott and Schafer, the best of the best quotes presented all in one tidy package. . . . The book invites taking back and forth from desk to bedside for endless dipping into for reading and then rereading, for sheer pleasure and painstaking insight. This book sparkles: as the title announces, with wit and with wisdom. This makes for a wondrous read, and feels like one's birthday."　　　　　　　　　　　　—Emanuel Hammer, PH.D.

"Would you like a pithy quote on transference? Feel all the good lines about caring in psychotherapy have been used? Gregory Bauer, in his new collection *Wit and Wisdom in Dynamic Psychotherapy*, proves for once and for all that our field has a treasure trove of quotes that is virtually inexhaustible. The book is organized around sixteen topics and the quotes are interesting, useful, and surprisingly readable, even as a continuous book. . . . It is an interesting, lively book that is worthwhile as a reference or to read as a text in psychotherapy."　　—Steven Ellman, PH.D.

"Gregory Bauer has put together an immensely useful, enlightening, and entertaining book. He has provided, in one volume, the most succinct and pertinent observations by psychoanalysts from Freud to Kernberg to Yalom, organized according to subjects such as 'Transference' and 'Resistance' and 'Change in Therapy' and 'Growing Up.' . . . His book is a treasure trove of insights—a veritable 'dictionary of famous quotes'—one every mental health professional will want at his or her fingertips. I highly recommend it."　　　　　　　—Gerald Schoenewolf, PH.D.

WIT
AND
WISDOM
IN
DYNAMIC
PSYCHOTHERAPY

Edited by

Gregory P. Bauer, Ph.D.

JASON ARONSON INC.
Northvale, New Jersey
London

Library of Congress Cataloging-in-Publication Data

Wit and wisdom in dynamic psychotherapy / edited by Gregory P. Bauer.
    p. cm.
  Includes bibliographical references.
  ISBN 0-87668-768-0
  1. Psychodynamic psychotherapy—Quotations, maxims, etc.
I. Bauer, Gregory P.
RC489.P72W57 1990
616.89'14—dc20   90-40191

Manufactured in the United States of America. Jason Aronson Inc. offers books and
cassettes. For information and catalog write to Jason Aronson Inc., 230 Livingston Street,
Northvale, New Jersey 07647.

TO KATHY, CARL, AND AARON

CONTENTS

PREFACE

This book brings together in one volume a collection of seminal observations concerning psychodynamic theory and practice. Throughout my training and clinical practice, I've always enjoyed the discovery of a comment or brief passage that captured the essence of a concept and clarified it in such a way that it became more easily absorbed and integrated. I've held dear these statements and find myself returning to them again and again, like old friends who assist me in sorting out my experiences in the consultation room. Over time, they have become part of how I view my world, my profession, and myself. Or perhaps I should say they've helped me clarify my views.

In preparing this offering I've cast the net broadly to include comments from some individuals not generally recognized as proponents of psychoanalytic theory. Though most of the quotes contained in this book are old favorites of mine, career-long companions, it also contains a sprinkling of new friends. Please note that no collection could possibly encompass the wealth of our field; this is but a sampling of what seems salient and of consequence.

In approaching these contributions the reader is asked to engage each quote fully, to sit with it and to allow its meaning to mingle with one's own understanding. Patience is encouraged because wisdom is not always on the surface. Readers will have to bring their own resources to plumb these gems; what escapes today may elicit a ring of recognition in a few months' time.

Gregory P. Bauer
Stevens Point, Wisconsin, 1990

It would be impossible to thank individually all those who have contributed to this book. Nevertheless, I would like to acknowledge my gratitude to those authors appearing in the bibliography, and to their publishers for extending permission to reprint. A special thanks is expressed to Jill Judd, whose warmth, diligence, and outstanding typing skills were critical in the preparation of this manuscript. An additional thanks is extended to Jason Aronson, M.D., for his enthusiasm, encouragement, and helpful suggestions.

To my wife, Kathy, and my sons, Carl and Aaron, I wish to express my thanks for their love, patience, and support.

WIT
AND
WISDOM
IN
DYNAMIC
PSYCHOTHERAPY

The
Analytic
Position

L ET US NOW glance at Freud's clinical setting. I will enumerate some of the very obvious points in its description.

1. At a stated time daily, five or six times a week, Freud put himself at the service of the patient. (This time was arranged to suit the convenience of both the analyst and the patient.)
2. The analyst would be reliably there, on time, alive, breathing.
3. For the limited period of time prearranged (about an hour) the analyst would keep awake and become preoccupied with the patient.
4. The analyst expressed love by the positive interest taken, and hate in the strict start and finish and in the matter of fees. Love and hate were honestly expressed, that is to say not denied by the analyst.
5. The aim of the analysis would be to get into touch with the process of the patient, to understand the material presented, to communicate this understanding in words. Resistance implied suffering and could be allayed by interpretation.
6. The analyst's method was one of objective observation.
7. This work was to be done in a room, not a passage, a room that was quiet and not liable to sudden unpredictable sounds, yet not dead quiet and not free from ordinary house noises. This room would be lit properly, but not by a light staring in the face, and not by a variable light. The room would certainly not be dark and it would

be comfortably warm. The patient would be lying on a couch, that is to say, comfortable, if able to be comfortable, and probably a rug and some water would be available.

8. The analyst (as is well known) keeps moral judgment out of the relationship, has no wish to intrude with details of the analyst's personal life and ideas, and the analyst does not wish to take sides in the persecutory systems even when these appear in the form of real shared situations, local, political, etc. Naturally if there is a war or an earthquake or if the king dies the analyst is not unaware.

9. In the analytic situation the analyst is much more reliable than people are in ordinary life, on the whole punctual, free from temper tantrums, free from compulsive falling in love, etc.

10. There is a very clear distinction in the analysis between fact and fantasy, so that the analyst is not hurt by an aggressive dream.

11. An absence of the talion reaction can be counted on.

12. The analyst survives.

D. W. Winnicott, 1955
pp. 20–21

THE PATIENT comes in from the street with its noises and voices and slowly glides into an atmosphere in which external reality is of no avail, where he hears only what his inner voices say, recollections and experiences, impulses and thoughts. He is himself, but he becomes more than the self he shows the world outside; that means he is entirely himself. The analyst is a certain Dr. A. or Dr. B., but at the same time he is also someone beyond this definite personality. He encompasses other figures beyond his own. He is a frame into which the patient puts a familiar picture, for the most part, a portrait of his family.

Theodor Reik, 1952
pp. 108–109

DURING THE analytic session the analyst shares with the patient this realm between fantasy and reality. He vicariously lives his patient's experiences and at the same time looks upon them with the factual regard of the investigator. He dives with the patient into the life of old and new experiences, but at every moment he is ready to regain the safe shore of psychological observation. It is his task to keep intact this character between reality and fantasy that is the essence of the analytic situation. This does not mean that he need do anything to promote the illusion; it only means that he must do nothing to disturb it.

Theodor Reik, 1952
pp. 111–112

IN THERAPY, as in dreaming sleep, we exclude the outside world; we keep things quiet, the door closed, and try not to interrupt the patient needlessly. . . . We try not to let our own opinions override the experience of the patient.

Sheldon Roth, 1987
p. 33

IN GENERAL, the more constant an environment remains, the more it fades into the background, so that the patient's inner imagination can come to the fore.

Sheldon Roth, 1987
p. 244

WE USED TO speak jokingly of the "Monday crust" when we began work again after the rest on Sunday. When the hours of work are less frequent, there is a risk of not being able to keep pace with the patient's

real life and of the treatment losing contact with the present and being
forced into by-paths.

Sigmund Freud, 1913
p. 127

⊒

LISTENING

THE ANALYST hears not only what is in the words; he also hears what
the words do not say. He listens with the "third ear," hearing not only
what the patient speaks but also his own inner voices, what emerges
from his own unconscious depths.

Theodor Reik, 1952
pp. 125–126

⊒

JUST AS THE patient must relate everything that his self-observation
can detect, and keep back all the logical and affective objections . . .
the doctor must put himself in a position to make use of everything he
is told for the purposes of interpretation and of recognizing the
concealed unconscious material. He must turn his own unconscious
like a receptive organ towards the transmitting unconscious of the
patient. He must adjust himself to the patient as a telephone receiver
is adjusted to the transmitting microphone.

Sigmund Freud, 1912b
p. 114

⊒

EVENLY SUSPENDED ATTENTION

. . . AS SOON AS anyone deliberately concentrates his attention to a
certain degree, he begins to select from the material before him; one
point will be fixed in his mind with particular clearness and some
other will be correspondingly disregarded, and in making this selection he will be following his expectations or inclinations. This how-

ever is precisely what must not be done. In making the selection, if he follows his expectations he is in danger of never finding anything but what he already knows; and if he follows his inclinations he will certainly falsify what he may perceive.

Sigmund Freud, 1912b
p. 112

目

As I HAD worked with this patient day by day, I had slowly built up within me a working model of the patient. . . . It is this working model which I now shifted into the foreground of my listening. I listened through this model.

Ralph Greenson, 1960
p. 421

目

The THERAPIST does not limit himself to the specific ideas, thoughts, or feelings produced by the patient at that particular moment, but instead he considers the full range of possible meanings, implications and connections that the patient's material brings to his mind. He permits his own thoughts and associations to range freely over this material, without rigidly preconceived ideas as to its meaning and significance, and he looks for connections or associations of which the patient may or may not have been conscious.

Paul Dewald, 1964
p. 175

目

An INTRICATE relationship exists between the capacity for surprise and the capacity to listen, for whenever one truly listens one exposes oneself to the possibility of surprise. If one does not want to be surprised, his best bet is not to listen, either to others or to himself.

Erwin Singer, 1965
p. 63

THE LUXURY of having someone listen to all that is said and treat it with regard, respect and interest is in itself a relatively unique phenomenon, and provides a significant gratification to the patient which is rarely offered in other human relationships.

Paul Dewald, 1964
p. 174

FROM MY encounters with patients I have learned an enormous amount, not just knowledge, but above all insight into my own nature. My patients brought me so close to the reality of human life that I could not help learning essential things from them. Encounters with people of so many different kinds and on so many different psychological levels have been for me incomparably more important than fragmentary conversations with celebrities. The finest and most significant conversations of my life were anonymous.

Carl Jung, 1961
p. 145

IT IS THE task of the analyst to transform the unconscious magical views of the patient into conscious psychological insight. In order to do this, the analyst cannot from the start deny or disavow the magical atmosphere in which the patient unconsciously lives. He must accept its psychical reality. To approach the unconscious processes in the spirit of cold, rational disavowal would be as stupid as it would be protest, "There are no ghosts!" when the ghost of the king appears in *Hamlet*. One must first accept and acknowledge the psychical reality of the apparition, otherwise it is not possible to understand what goes on in Hamlet's mind. In this recognition, the audience follows the advice of the prince himself. When the ghost speaks, Horatio cries, "O day and night, but this is wondrous strange!" And Hamlet answers, "And therefore as a stranger give it welcome." It is in this spirit of preliminary acceptance that analysts listen to the voice of unconscious processes.

Theodor Reik, 1952
p. 112

己

IT IS THE task of the analyst to bring into consciousness that which is unconscious, no matter to which psychic institution it belongs. He directs his attention equally and objectively to the unconscious elements in all three institutions. . . . When he sets about the work of enlightenment, he takes his stand at a point equidistant from the id, the ego, and the superego.

Anna Freud, 1966
p. 28

己

NEUTRALITY

ONE OF THE rules of analyzing is that one should not take sides in the analysand's conflicts.

Roy Schafer, 1983
p. 74

己

THE MORE active and forceful the therapist (even if ostensibly in the service of helping the patient assume responsibility), the more is the patient infantilized.

Irvin Yalom, 1980
p. 267

Neutrality does not mean an avoidance of doing anything, but rather giving equal attention to all the patient's productions, without prior weighting of one kind of material over another, and confining oneself to the analytic task, that is, abstaining from deliberate suggestion.

Merton Gill, 1982
p. 63

己

... Neutrality does not preclude an empathic, authentic, warm attitude on the part of the therapist, but, to the contrary, may best reflect such warmth and empathy under conditions in which the emergence of the patient's regressive aggression in the transference would naturally bring about counteraggressive reactions in the therapist. The therapist's emotional capacity to maintain an empathic attitude in such circumstances (the therapist's "holding" action) and his cognitive capacity to integrate ("contain") the fragmentarily expressed transferences are important components of such technical neutrality.

Otto Kernberg, 1982
p. 33

己

It is not a departure from neutrality to call a spade a spade.

Roy Schafer, 1983
p. 6

己

Lack of emotional responsiveness, silence, the pretense of being an inhuman computer-like machine which gathers data and emits interpretations do no more supply the psychological milieu for the most undistorted delineation of the normal and abnormal features of a person's psychological makeup than do an oxygen-free atmosphere and a temperature close to the zero-point supply the physical milieu for the most accurate measurement of his physiological responses. Appropriate neutrality in the analytic situation is provided by average conditions. The analyst's behavior vis-à-vis his patient should be the expected average one—i.e., the behavior of a psychologically percep- tive person vis-à-vis someone who is suffering and has entrusted himself to him for help.

Heinz Kohut, 1977
p. 253

⊐

THREE VALUES, the love of truth, the ethic of personal freedom, and the analyst's caring commitment to the patient, are implicit in the analyst's neutral attitudes and techniques. . . . The analyst should seek and speak the truth; he should have a caring commitment to the patient, and he should respect the patient's freedom.

Theodore Dorpat, 1977
p. 58

⊐

ANALYTIC neutrality does not mean . . . indifference to or nonin- volvement with the destructive aspects of acting-out behavior. The analyst should first attempt to deal with acting out by interpreting the motives, defenses, conflicts, or other relevant aspects of the behavior. If meaningful and effective interpretive work cannot be accomplished, then the therapist should confront the patient with the destructive implications and consequences of the acting out.

Theodore Dorpat, 1977
p. 44

⊐

I TRY NOT to take sides in any of his conflicts except that I am working against his resistances, against his damaging neurotic behavior, and against his self-destructiveness.

Ralph Greenson, 1967
p. 216

Owing to his or her recognition that over the course of an analysis the analysand will present highly selective and changing pictures of other people, the neutral analyst remains nonjudgmental. . . . It is particularly important to maintain this neutrality in relation to parental figures and spouses, for to some extent the analysand is identified with them and is vulnerable to the same value judgments that may be passed on them.

Roy Schafer, 1983
p. 151

己

. . . As an analysis progresses, the pictures of parents tend to change radically, especially in the direction of complexity and conflictedness.

Roy Schafer, 1983
p. 151

己

. . . If a critical judgment can be made about someone else, then it is possible that, at some time, it can also be made about the patient.

Peter Giovacchini, 1979
p. 446

己

Resident: Should I apologize for what I did, or rather what I didn't do—that is, listen to what he had to say without judging him prematurely?

Supervisor: Don't burden him with your confession. It's not his function to forgive you. You probably feel worse about it now than he does. The best thing you can do is just get to work with him and show him that you are ready to deal with whatever comes up—if not the first time, then the next time around.

Michael Basch, 1980
p. 101

Psychoanalytic neutrality facilitates transference by frustrating the patient's wishes for transference gratification and by providing the conditions for making it safe for the patient to experience and express his transferences.

Theodore Dorpat, 1977
p. 46

🮱

Repressed sexual fantasies towards therapist and parents can become conscious if the patient feels safe enough with the therapist.

Harry Guntrip, 1969
p. 334

🮱

It is, therefore, just as disastrous for the analysis if the patient's craving for love is gratified as it is if it is suppressed. The course the analyst must pursue is neither of these; it is one for which there is no model in real life. He must take care not to steer away from the transference-love, or to repulse it or to make it distasteful to the patient; but he must just as resolutely withhold any response to it. . . . The more plainly the analyst lets it be seen that he is proof against every temptation, the more readily will he be able to extract from the situation its analytic content.

Sigmund Freud, 1915
p. 166

🮱

The patient then unconsciously set out to determine whether or not the analyst would reciprocate his interest. The patient's testing of the neutral analyst assured him that he could not seduce the analyst. Assured that it would be safe for him to experience his erotic interest, he lifted his defenses and permitted it to awareness. Patients . . . may wish for what they do not want. The patient wanted mastery and understanding, not gratification of his wishes.

Theodore Dorpat, 1977
p. 47

⊒

FREE ASSOCIATION, recall, and self-revelation are . . . contingent upon complete trust, specifically the sense that self-esteem will not be shattered by disapproval and rejection. It is as if the courage to face himself depends on the patient's conviction that the therapist can bear the patient's revelations without anxiety and defenses of his own.

Erwin Singer, 1965
p. 180

⊒

FRUSTRATION

IN ORDER FOR a neurotic to realize the intensity or enormity of his childish desires these desires must be permitted to reach a certain level of insistence. Without this pressure of insistence any interpretive effort is doomed to failure. This is the frustration imposed on patients in analysis or intensive psychotherapy. Without frustration in the therapeutic situation and under the conditions of the therapist gratifying the wishes of the patient, the relationship is closer to an adoption than to therapy. However, some of this adoption may be necessary under certain conditions.

Sidney Tarachow, 1963
p. 274

⊒

THE ANALYTIC situation is thus a paradox: it stimulates, and at the same time frustrates, the development of an intense human relationship. In a sense, analyst and patient tease each other. The analytic situation requires that each participant have strong experiences, and yet not act on them. Perhaps this is one of the reasons that not only many patients, but also many therapists, cannot stand it: they prefer to seek encounters that are less taxing emotionally, or that offer better opportunities for discharging affective tensions in action.

Thomas Szasz, 1963
p. 437

ᘒ

O<small>N THE ONE</small> hand, this absence of a response in the therapist becomes a source of frustration for the patient, in that the drive-derivatives become increasingly manifest and conscious, but cannot be satisfied. At the same time, however, this lack of responsiveness is a source of reassurance, in that it permits the patient an opportunity to express the feelings and fantasies previously warded off, without having to take immediate responsibility for them, or to be afraid that they will lead to some type of immediate act.

Paul Dewald, 1964
p. 197

ᘒ

T<small>HE STATE OF</small> abstinence, then, refers to the activity of both patient and analyst: the analyst must abstain from responding to the patient's pleas, charges, maneuvers, requests, and demands in the way he would ordinarily respond were this a social relationship, and the patient must experience the denied satisfaction. For so far we have come upon no better method for allowing the patient to discover his style of, and his conditions for, loving and hating. It is this controlled frustration in analysis that highlights the patient's typical methods of relating himself to the significant people in his life. This self-discovery is crucial for the process of recovery.

Karl Menninger, 1958
p. 57

AT THE VERY outset the analyst denies himself the patient as a real object. The patient, on the other hand, *begins* therapy with the therapist as a real object and must slowly learn to deny himself that gratification and so establish the necessary preconditions for the transference *as if*.

Sidney Tarachow, 1963
p. 14

AN UNINTERPRETED *relationship to the therapist is real, as real as any other relationship.* The interposition of the *as if* problem creates a state of tension and deprivation which is the kernel of the therapeutic task. The degree to which this task is imposed will depend on the therapist's evaluation of the patient's capabilities.

Sidney Tarachow, 1963
p. 10

THE THERAPEUTIC task for the therapist is with his own struggle with his need for objects and with the self-imposed therapeutic barrier. The temptation to breach the barrier will assail the therapist at all times. If the patient pleads for help, the therapist wants to extend himself, if the patient is hostile, the therapist wants to fight. The therapist's task is to restrain himself from regarding these phenomena as real and thus destroying the transference *as if* potential. This restraint separates him from the patient as object and imposes upon the analyst the task of tolerating loneliness.

Sidney Tarachow, 1963
p. 13

No ONE LIKES to hurt people—to cause them pain, to stand silently by as they suffer, to withhold help from them when they plead for it. That's where the real wear and tear of analysis lies—in this chronic struggle to keep oneself from doing the things that decent people naturally and spontaneously do. One hears a lot about the abstinence that the analytic patient has to endure, but the abstinence of the analyst is more ruthless and corrosive.

Janet Malcolm, 1981
p. 77

THE TASK OF setting aside the other as a real object I regard as the central problem in the theory of the treatment process.

Sidney Tarachow, 1963
p. 377

... OBJECT HUNGER is as much a problem of the therapist's as it is the patient's. This hunger must be set aside by both to establish the conditions for transference neurosis and analytic work.

Sidney Tarachow, 1963
p. 17

THE THERAPEUTIC task can be imposed only by means of a disappointment and by transformation of a real into an *as if* relationship. We force thinking in place of reality; the uninterpreted relationship is reality.

Sidney Tarachow, 1963
p. 14

IF THE THERAPIST treats his patient as real, he is using the patient to overcome his own sense of loneliness and sense of abandonment by his original symbiotic object.

Sidney Tarachow, 1963
p. 15

⊇

IN ANALYSIS, IT is best for the patient if one approaches *everything* analytically. It is as important to understand why a patient is closely "allied" with his analyst in the analytic work as it is to understand why there seems to be no "alliance" at all.

Charles Brenner, 1979
p. 150

⊇

IT IS TRUE enough that it often does no harm for an analyst to be thus conventionally "human." Still, there are times when his being "human" under such circumstances can be harmful, and one cannot always know in advance when those times will be. As an example, for his analyst to express sympathy for a patient who has just lost a close relative may make it more difficult than it would otherwise be for the patient to express pleasure or spite or exhibitionistic satisfaction over the loss.

Charles Brenner, 1979
p. 153

⊇

I STRONGLY advise against any attempt on the part of the psychiatrist to make things seemingly easier for the patient by pretending that the professional doctor–patient relationship is a social one. Deep down in his mind, no patient wants a nonprofessional relationship with his therapist, regardless of the fact that he may express himself to the contrary.

Frieda Fromm-Reichmann, 1950
p. 46

... T HE PSYCHIATRIST should never feel called upon to be anything more or less than the participant observer of the emotional experiences which are conveyed to him by his patients.

Frieda Fromm-Reichmann, 1950
p. 41

⊐

A DDITIONALLY, the analyst is not constrained to respond overtly in the ordinary social way and so may, and usually will, defer response while sorting out what is essential, timely, basic, or authentic.

Roy Schafer, 1983
p. 38

⊐

SILENCE

T HE ACTIVE power of silence makes small talk transparent and has a force that pulls the patient forward, driving him into deeper layers than he intended.

Theodor Reik, 1952
p. 124

⊐

T HE POSITIVE aspect of silence in a treatment is hard to *prescribe* for oneself, to *teach* to others, and it is hard to *communicate* its importance to patients who fear lack of verbiage in the hours. Encouraging experience of the nonverbal is the reciprocal of encouraging free association. In music we gain a sense of rhythm through the absence of sound. A similar process occurs in communication between two people. In teaching students a feeling for the correct dosage of verbal interpretations, I often use the metaphor of a pond. Toss one stone into it and rhythmic, harmonic waves emanate from the center of the site. A second stone may do more of the same with some overlap. But throw one stone too many, and the rhythmic organized waves become turbulent and chaotic. The pond needs to rest. The dosage of silence is harder to teach than the dosage of words: it is hard to learn and bear the uncertain consequences of silence in daily practice.

Sheldon Roth, 1987
p. 226

⊇

THE SPOKEN word has a reactive effect upon the speaker. The silence of the analyst intensifies this reaction; it functions as a sounding board.

Theodor Reik, 1952
p. 124

⊇

SIMILARLY, IT is not unusual for therapists to use speech as an activity defense. The tensions that exist between patient and therapist are emotionally palpable during silences, especially after the crystalliza-tion of the clinical transference. Rather than bearing the uncertain consequences of prolonged silence, many therapists will break silence (transferential tension) with questions and comments that in effect serve as reassurances, whatever their content. Although this speech may be indicated in certain cases, mental states, or clinical emergen-cies, as a repeated pattern it places the patient in a passive position. It is misleading to suggest to the patient that the therapist can perform the therapy.

Sheldon Roth, 1987
p. 228

⊇

TO REMAIN silent when one is asked a question, for example, is not neutral but rude. It goes without saying that—given specific clinical circumstances, and after appropriate explanations—there are moments in analysis when the analyst will not pretend to respond to the patient's pseudorealistic requests but will instead insist on the investigation of their transference meaning.

Heinz Kohut, 1971
p. 39

コ

SILENCE AT THE BEGINNING OF AN HOUR

W HAT WE are always striving for is to be at the edge of the patient's most immediate experience and awareness. When our patient walks through the door we have no real idea of what this might be. We want to behave as if excessive movement puts all of living nature into hiding, as it does at a woodland pond.

Sheldon Roth, 1987
p. 229

コ

N O MATTER how deep the patient's confidence in the analyst, his acceptance seems less born of "confidence" than of the fact that the doctor spoke to him with candor about things that mattered. The therapist was not "clever" but to the point, was not dazzling but unmasking. What undoubtedly impressed the patient was the therapist's courage to see, his honesty in telling, and his willingness to accept the patient despite what he saw. And so the point is not how much positive transference *has* been established, but how much genuine rather than irrational respect *is* established—and forthright confrontations establish rational respect.

Erwin Singer, 1965
p. 215

コ

T HE PATIENTS will stay if they feel that they can trust their problems to you. They will stay if they feel that you have gotten these issues from them in a sympathetic and friendly way, and that basically you have sympathy for them and for humanity. They will know it, they will sense it, and they will give you tremendous confidences, and they will come back and face you again.

Sidney Tarachow, 1963
p. 172

⊒

HUMOR

SOMETIMES humor expresses true warmth and affection. At other times it is used to mask hostility behind a false facade of camaraderie or to blunt the sharpness of disagreement. . . . Even in social situations humor is not always kind. And since both kinds of humor can occur simultaneously, it is not always easy to be sure which is dominant.

Lawrence Kubie, 1971
pp. 861–862

⊒

THE THERAPIST must always remember that he is rarely the first person who has found something "amusing" in the patient's life, in his idiosyncratic patterns of speech and behavior, or in his symptoms. . . . Some of the most destructive people in the story of a patient's life may have been those who always found something to smile about whenever the patient was in pain.

Lawrence Kubie, 1971
p. 863

⊒

A SPECIAL warning is in order against . . . bitter banter. . . . Here the therapist indulges a fantasy that he has a license to attack under a thin disguise of humor.

Lawrence Kubie, 1971
p. 866

⊒

I‍T DOES NOT follow . . . that the therapist should never tell the patient
a joke or engage in a humorous interchange. This would be a stiffly
wooden and unnatural relationship in a situation where two human
beings are together for a long period of time. Sometimes, telling a joke
or an anecdote illuminates an interpretation in a way that the patient
can understand; and the art of therapy, just as the art of any effective
communication, is in knowing how to present material that can be
grasped clearly by the other person.

Richard Chessick, 1980
p. 42

⊐

H‍UMOR CONVEYS a sense of dignity and hints at a civilized relationship with the listening therapist, for it implies mutual understanding.
Once, as a patient lay down on the couch to begin an analysis, he said:
"psychoanalysis is like marriage. It's something you hope you have to
do only once." . . . The humor revealed his observing ego, which took
some distance from experience of himself, and suggested his capacity
for reflective self-observation. It helped make the unbearable bearable,
which, after all, is much of what the psychotherapeutic process is all
about.

Sheldon Roth, 1987
pp. 104–105

⊐

RESPECT

R‍ESPECT IS conveyed by means of all aspects of the therapist's
behavior and has its basis in the therapist's self-respect.

Hans Strupp and Jeffrey Binder, 1984
p. 46

Every self-analysis that leads into a certain depth convinces the analyst that there is no basic psychological difference between him and the patients he is treating. An occasional blind date with oneself is here recommended to the analyst, not only as a way to enlarge the knowledge of his own personality but also as an excellent method of self-education. Many analysts are inclined to exaggerate in their thoughts the distance that separates them from their neurotic and psychotic patients. Nothing but luck has decided that we are on this side of the fence and not on the other or that we are sitting behind the couch and not on it. Where this sober insight threatens to lose its strength, self-analysis will restore it.

Theodor Reik, 1952
p. 59

... The first prerequisite for successful psychotherapy is the respect that the psychiatrist must extend to the mental patient. Such respect can be valid only if the psychiatrist realizes that his patient's difficulties in living are not too different from his own.

Frieda Fromm-Reichmann, 1951
p. xi

The more the analyst's technique and behaviour are suggestive of omniscience and omnipotence, the greater is the danger of a malig-nant form of regression. On the other hand, the more the analyst can reduce the inequality between his patient and himself, and the more unobtrusive and ordinary he can remain in his patient's eyes, the better are the chances of a benign form. ...

Michael Balint, 1968
p. 173

Iтs GOOD FOR both patient and therapist to be reminded periodically that the problematic areas of life don't represent the sum total of a person's existence. It helps counteract the notion that the patient is a helpless, crippled individual who needs to lean on the wise, strong therapist. Often patients are quite competent individuals who happen to have trouble applying what they know to a particular aspect of their lives. Sometimes the therapist may even have to face the fact that on balance he is less mature and effective than a given patient. But that doesn't preclude the patient's needing the therapist's help or the therapist's being able to assist the patient.

Michael Basch, 1980
pp. 103–104

⊒

Iɴ ALL YOUR dealings with the patient, be realistic. Convey by word and action that there are many things you cannot do and you are not interested in attempting. Patients will idealize the therapist (as a reflection of their own perceived neediness and helplessness) and then take delight in demonstrating that their idol has clay feet.

Hans Strupp and Jeffrey Binder, 1984
p. 49

⊒

Iғ THE ANALYST assumes actively the role of "prophet, saviour and redeemer," he actively encourages conflict solution by gross identification, but stands in the way of the patient's gradual integration of his own psychological structures and of the gradual building up of new ones.

Heinz Kohut, 1971
p. 165

Mɪɢʜᴛ ɪ ᴘᴇʀʜᴀᴘs have kept the girl under my treatment if I myself had acted a part, if I had exaggerated personal interest in her — a course which, even after allowing for my position as her physician, would have been tantamount to providing her with a substitute for the affection she longed for? I do not know. . . . I have always avoided acting a part, and have contented myself with practising the humbler arts of psychology. In spite of every theoretical interest and of every endeavor to be of assistance as a physician, I keep the fact in mind that there must be some limits set to the extent to which psychological influence may be used. . . .

Sigmund Freud, 1905a
p. 109

Tʜus ᴛʜᴇ analyst's modesty must be no studied pose, but a reflection of the limitation of our knowledge.

Sandor Ferenczi, 1928
p. 94

Hᴏᴡᴇᴠᴇʀ much the analyst may be tempted to become a teacher, model and ideal for other people and to create men in his own image, he should not forget that that is not his task in the analytic relationship, and indeed that he will be disloyal to his task if he allows himself to be led on by his inclinations. If he does, he will only be repeating a mistake of the parents who crushed their child's independence by their influence, and he will only be replacing the patient's earlier dependence by a new one.

Sigmund Freud, 1940
p. 175

T HE PATIENT was silent and then he laughed. . . . I asked what he thought the laugh meant. He said he was pleased by my attitude. "You leave everything as it is. You illuminate. You do not try to control or change anything."

Theodore Dorpat, 1977
p. 53

⊒

A UTONOMY is to be protected and preserved.

Gertrude and Rubin Blanck, 1974
p. 119

⊒

. . . T HE THERAPIST should resist the compulsion to do something, especially at those times when he or she feels under pressure from the patient (and him or herself) to intervene, perform, reassure, and so on.

Hans Strupp and Jeffrey Binder, 1984
p. 41

⊒

I N THERAPY THE patient strives mightily to coax or persuade the therapist to make decisions for him or her; and one of the therapist's chief tasks is to resist being manipulated into taking care of, or taking over, the patient. To manipulate the therapist, a patient may exaggerate helplessness or withhold evidence of strengths. . . . Many patients caught in a decisional crisis scan the therapist's every syllable, gesture, or shift of posture as though each were the expression of an oracle; they rummage about in their postsession recollections of the therapist's words in search of clues to the latter's view of the proper decision. Regardless of their level of sophistication, patients secretly yearn for the therapist who will provide structure and guidance. The anger and the frustration that at some level occurs in every course of therapy stems from the patient's dawning recognition that the therapist will not relieve him or her of the burden of decision.

Irvin Yalom, 1980
p. 324

⊇

By ANSWERING rather than analyzing the question, the analyst unconsciously acted out the omnipotent role attributed to him by the patient.

Theodore Dorpat, 1977
p. 49

⊇

In THE LONG run, the patient appreciates it if the psychiatrist does not comply with his request for direct practical advice, no matter how much he may be pressing the doctor for it at the time. His innate tendency toward health, growth, and maturation will eventually be greater than his time-bound wish for the type of help and advice that may interfere with his motivation toward health and independence.

Frieda Fromm-Reichmann, 1950
p. 209

⊇

ADVICE IS free (and worth it). . . .

Kenneth Colby, 1958
p. 12

⊇

It IS MOST important for the novice psychotherapist to understand that in choosing to influence or educate a patient directly, he is also making an implicit decision about the patient's potential for maturity. Assuming that the decision to influence the patient directly is not made on the basis of a countertransference problem of the therapist — which is usually the reason — the decision implies that the patient must be treated as a child with little potential for autonomous growth, and therefore, direct modification is the most we can hope for, switching the patient's dependency from the parents to us. This may be a legitimate technique providing we have a thorough metapsychological understanding of the patient and have given the patient every chance to realize his potential. . . . Massive attempts to educate and influence a patient directly do not represent "kindness" but rather an expression of therapeutic despair.

Richard Chessick, 1980
pp. 182–183

戸

THE VIEWPOINT that direct teaching is not an effective tool for people with psychological problems is based on the observation that the patient cannot really utilize directions and advice because he needs his problems for his psychological economy. They serve a purpose and are not simply noxious as he wishes to believe.

Ernst Beier, 1966
p. 76

戸

BY COMMANDS and prohibitions all that we do is really only to relieve the patient's ego from assuming its responsibilities.

Franz Alexander, 1925
p. 494

Resident: I was wondering whether I should advise him to see more people, make an effort to get out. Human contact seems to help him so much.

Supervisor: Don't spoil good therapy. He'll find his way once he is free to do so. Your job is first of all to try to understand him, which you are doing with good results, and then to help him understand himself.

Michael Basch, 1980
p. 93

⊐

In the long run the ex-patient finds his own attachments and commitments

Karl Menninger, 1958
p. 94

⊐

CARING

The therapist's caring should be indestructible and not dependent upon reciprocal caring by the patient.

Irvin Yalom, 1980
p. 409

⊐

. . . The mature therapist will care despite rebelliousness, narcissism, depression, hostility, and mendacity. In fact, one might say that the therapist cares *because* of these traits, since they reflect how much the individual needs to be cared for.

Irvin Yalom, 1980
p. 408

T HE PSYCHOANALYST'S caring is not so much a feeling as it is an attitude and a commitment. Therapists cannot maintain and should not be expected to have any particular feeling or emotion for the patient. Feelings come and go; a commitment endures.

Theodore Dorpat, 1977
p. 60

己

W ILL THE patient ask, "Do you love me?" "If you really care for me, would you see me if I had no money?" "Is therapy really a purchased relationship?" It is true that these questions veer perilously close to that ultimate secret of the psychotherapist which is that the encounter with the patient plays a relatively small role in the therapist's overall life. . . . Indeed, this denial of specialness is one of the cruel truths and poorly kept secrets of therapy: the patient has one therapist; the therapist, many patients. The therapist is far more important to the patient than the patient to the therapist. To my mind there is only one response that therapists can make to such questions from patients: that when the therapist is with the patient, he or she is fully with the patient; the therapist strives to give his or her entire presence to the other.

Irvin Yalom, 1980
p. 415

己

MONEY

P SYCHO-ANALYSIS is often reproached with being remarkably concerned with money matters. My own opinion is that is is far too little concerned with them. Even the most prosperous individual spends money on doctors most unwillingly. Something in us seems to make us regard medical aid, which in fact we all first received from our mothers in infancy, as something to which we are automatically entitled, and at the end of each month, when our patients are presented with their bill, their resistance is stimulated into producing all their concealed or unconscious hatred, mistrust, and suspicion over again. The most characteristic example of the contrast between conscious generosity and concealed resentment was given by the patient who opened the conversation by saying: "Doctor, if you help me, I'll give you every penny I possess!" "I shall be satisfied with thirty kronen an hour," the physician replied. "But isn't that rather excessive?" the patient unexpectedly remarked.

Sandor Ferenczi, 1928
pp. 92–93

⊒

BEGINNING therapists sometimes tend to be self-abnegating about the fee. It is useful for them to know that the fee is the only part of the therapy that is legitimately for the therapist. If one is clear about this and establishes an adequate fee, there is less temptation to desire other compensations from the patient. The therapist who is adequately paid for his services is less likely to need positive transference manifestations, gifts, and other tokens of love.

Gertrude and Rubin Blanck, 1974
p. 173

⊒

ONE'S FINANCIAL arrangements should not be presented to a patient as if they were motivated by the patient's therapeutic needs.

Sheldon Roth, 1987
p. 249

⊒

MUCH CAN BE learned about a person's psychic life if we observe how he handles money.

Thomas Paolino, 1981
p. 169

... M ONEY MATTERS ARE treated by civilized people in the same way as sexual matters—with the same inconsistency, prudishness, and hypocrisy.

Sigmund Freud, 1913
p. 131

⊒

R EMUNERATION for services is a generally accepted convention in our society, yet there appears to be a feeling among many people that some services deserve payment more than others. Few people would argue that the TV repairman should "forget" his bill and be content with the fact that he is providing pleasure for them.

Ernst Beier, 1966
p. 96

⊒

I T SHOULD BE remembered that he is not paying money for relief; relief is what he wants, but what he pays for are the professional services of the physician.

Karl Menninger, 1958
p. 28

⊒

O RDINARY good sense cautions him, furthermore, not to allow large sums of money to accumulate, but to ask for payment at fairly short regular intervals — monthly, perhaps. (It is a familiar fact that the value of the treatment is not enhanced in the patient's eyes if a very low fee is asked.)

Sigmund Freud, 1913
p. 13

THE MONEY paid by a patient to a psychoanalyst is *not* in payment for the analyst's "time." Many psychiatrists fall into an error of thinking in this regard. Time is not for sale; it belongs to the universe, not to the physician. The physician may measure the price of her services by the clock, but this is merely a convenience. He is no more selling "his" time than is a silk merchant selling "his" yards. He is selling his professional services for so and so long a period.

Karl Menninger, 1958
p. 28

⊐

REASSURANCE

IT IS THE task of therapy to bring out the patient's anxieties and trace them to their origin, not to drive them underground by reassuring them.

David Malan, 1979
p. 77

⊐

MANY PSYCHOTHERAPISTS try to achieve their effect by "augmenting the patient's self-confidence." Since self-confidence generally diminishes anxiety, this would actually be a good device. . . . However, an attempt at augmenting self-confidence by suggestion is a two-edged sword. If a patient has self-confidence because a doctor has told him to have it, he has more confidence in the doctor than in himself. The self-confidence is a borrowed one and is lost again when the participation in the doctor's power is lost.

Otto Fenichel, 1945
pp. 563–564

In TEACHING psycho-analysis we must continue to speak against reassurance. As we look a little more carefully, however, we see that this is too simple. . . . It is not just a question of reassurance and no reassurance. In fact, the whole matter needs examination. What is a reassurance? What could be more reassuring than to find oneself being well analysed, to be in a reliable setting with a mature person in charge, capable of making penetrating and accurate interpretation, and to find one's personal process respected? it is foolish to deny that reassurance is present in the classical analytic situation. The whole set-up of psycho-analysis is one big reassurance, especially the reliable objectivity and behaviour of the analyst, and the transference interpretations constructively using instead of wastefully exploiting the moment's passion.

D. W. Winnicott, 1955
p. 25

ANONYMITY

The DOCTOR should be opaque to his patients and, like a mirror, should show them nothing but what is shown to him.

Sigmund Freud, 1912b
p. 118

If THE ANALYST remains under the illusion that the current cues he provides to the patient can be reduced to the vanishing point, he may be led into a silent withdrawal, which is not too distant from the caricature of an analyst as someone who does indeed refuse to have any personal relationship with the patient. What happens then is that silence has become a technique rather than merely an indication that the analyst is listening.

Merton Gill, 1979
p. 277

I DOUBT THAT the evolution of the transference neurosis is often seriously disturbed by the patient's knowing whether one takes one's vacation in Vermont or Maine, or indeed (let me be really bold!) that one knows something more about sailing than about golf or bridge.

Leo Stone, 1961
p. 48

己

W HAT ANONYMITY should mean is that the therapist will make every effort to maintain the focus on the patient's life and problems.

Steven Levy, 1984
p. 126

己

W E CANNOT ignore the fact that what the psychoanalyst believes, what he lives for, what he loves, what he considers to be the purpose of life and the joy of life, what he considers to be good and what he considers to be evil, become known to the patient and influence him enormously not as "suggestion" but as inspiration.

Karl Menninger, 1958
p. 91

己

A PATIENT begins his session with "how do you do?" He says a few words about the happenings of today or yesterday, but within a few minutes they are forgotten and the past becomes as vivid as if it were the present. Parents, long dead, come alive again in his memory, childhood scenes are reexperienced as if they were here and now and early sorrows are felt as if today had brought them forth. Rage and love, hate and tenderness, are freely expressed and thoughts that shy away from the light of the day creep out of their hiding-places. And then comes the moment when the self-induced spell is broken. The patient gets up from the couch and sees only the actual consultation room. He must make a sudden emotional readjustment upon finding himself again in the world of reality.

Theodor Reik, 1952
p. 109

2

The
First
Hour

Lᴇᴛ ᴜs ʙᴇɢɪɴ our discussion of the initial interview with its end. The last question I pose at the end of a first meeting is, "Will you be satisfied after you leave that I have grasped and appreciated what you wanted me to know about you, or will you feel that I have missed something essential?"

Sheldon Roth, 1987
p. 77

⊒

Tʜᴇ ɪɴɪᴛɪᴀʟ meeting of therapist and patient poses several important problems. The most immediate question is, of course, the definition of their relationship to each other.

Erwin Singer, 1965
p. 125

⊒

Aꜱ ɪ ꜱᴇᴇ it, such an interview is a situation of . . . communication . . . on a progressively unfolding *expert–client* basis for the purpose of elucidating characteristic *patterns of living* of the subject person, the

patient or client, which patterns he experiences as particularly troublesome or especially valuable, and in the revealing of which he expects
to derive *benefit*.

Harry Stack Sullivan, 1954
p. 4

THE TRADITIONAL psychiatric interview was modeled after the general
medical interview, separated into history taking and mental-status
examination. . . . Under the influence of psychoanalytic theory and
practice, the traditional psychiatric interview gradually changed,
shifting the emphasis to the patient–interviewer interaction. It replaced a semistandard sequence of questions with a more flexible
evaluation of the predominant problems, focused on the patient's
understanding of his conflicts, and linked the study of the patient's
personality to that of his present behavior in the interview.

Otto Kernberg, 1977
p. 92

THERE ARE . . . people to whom it is so very easy to talk that you say
a good deal more than you ever intended to say, and if you stop to
consider why, you will usually find that each topic grew "naturally"
out of that which preceded. Or if events did not proceed in the most
"natural" way, then there was very probably a quite careful attention
to transitions, so that you were never surprised. The questions which
were asked seemed to be the right, sensible ones, and the other person
seemed always to show a rather sensitive comprehension of what you
were attempting to evoke in his mind; and so it was very easy to go on
and on.

Harry Stack Sullivan, 1954
p. 209

THE CHIEF handicap to communication is anxiety. There are times when anxiety on the part of the interviewee is unavoidable or even necessary, but in general an important part of the psychiatrist's work is his use of skill to avoid unnecessary anxiety.

Harry Stack Sullivan, 1954
p. 206

己

FURTHERMORE, when . . . anxiety makes it impossible for the patient to go any further in a particular direction—when you see that his tension is increasing to the point of interfering with communication— you will find it wise to move emphatically out of the particular topic which is being discussed into another. Perhaps you can come back to it later. As a matter of fact, most topics of human living are so interlocked that you can approach the same thing from six or seven different directions.

Harry Stack Sullivan, 1954
p. 211

己

IT HAS BEEN my experience that one way of minimizing anxiety about the initial clinical encounter is to realize that my first job is to get acquainted with the patient. . . . Rather than focusing exclusively on a symptom or complaint per se, I make it my business to learn something about the person in whom the problem resides.

Michael Basch, 1980
p. 3

己

NEVER LET A patient present himself as exclusively negative: he also has to face what is good about himself. Surprisingly it is sometimes harder to get a patient to "confess" to his assets than to his faults.

Behind this is the patient's nonconscious intent to seek a regressive solution for his problems. If he can paint himself as all bad and incompetent then it is up to the doctor to rescue him. Once he faces his assets as well as his liabilities he has to accept the fact that, with whatever aid the therapist can give him he is potentially capable of doing something for himself.

Michael Basch, 1980
p. 24

ℤ

THE USE OF QUESTIONS

. . . WHEN YOU actively gather information which you plan to use only at some future time, you necessarily incur the undesirable side effects of the interviewing format. The major one is the expectation on the patient's part that once you have amassed all the necessary information about him, you will proceed to give him useful interpretations.

I. H. Paul, 1978
p. 139

ℤ

HOW ONE proceeds to review a patient's life depends on the intensity of his present problems and the need for immediate reduction of anxiety. This will determine how quickly one can move toward an anamnestic review of the patient's past life or whether time will have to be spent on issues related to his present living.

Leon Salzman, 1980
p. 269

ℤ

USHERING A frightened stranger into an office and expecting him to know what to do without explanation is a caricature of analytic technique and is never appropriate even if, and especially if, the patient has been in therapy before or is a therapist himself. Nothing need be or should be assumed, an attitude that will characterize the therapist's position throughout the treatment.

Steven Levy, 1984
p. 9

己

IN PRINCIPLE, the therapist should try to help the patient describe his problems in his own way, with as few questions and structuring remarks as possible.

Steven Levy, 1984
p. 10

己

IF THE THERAPIST has information about the patient from another source (i.e., a referring clinician), it is important to indicate this to the patient. . . . Any outside information, that is, facts the patient has not himself told the therapist, must be brought into the treatment. The patient must feel he is in charge of what he reveals about himself and should not have to wonder what his therapist already knows.

Steven Levy, 1984
p. 8

己

THE THERAPIST cannot afford to be stampeded into activity by demands that he do something about the patient's immediate complaints.

Michael Basch, 1980
p. 170

IF THE THERAPIST feels under pressure to arrive at a quick under-standing of the patient's problems—especially, to "do" something about them—the assessment process will assume an unduly narrow form.

Hans Strupp and Jeffrey Binder, 1984
p. 52

ⴲ

IN DEALING WITH people, one must realize that there are always reser-vations in communication—things that all of us are taught from the cradle onward as dangerous to even think about, much less to communicate freely about. Thus the interviewer recognizes automat-ically, and as a preliminary to all communication, that no one will be simply "frank"; such a phenomenon . . . does not describe interper-sonal relations.

Harry Stack Sullivan, 1954
p. 206

ⴲ

THE THERAPIST . . . threatens the patient's present state of adjustment by the very fact that he holds out his service as a therapist. . . .

Ernst Beier, 1966
p. 120

ⴲ

ONE OF THE most common presentations seen in medicine: aches and pains for which little basis in physical disorder can be found. The next step, too often neglected, is for someone to take the trouble to see if a painful life might explain the pains in the body.

James Gustafson, 1986
p. 151

DIAGNOSIS

... I BELIEVE THAT the usefulness of classification from a therapeutic perspective is extremely limited. In my mind, Freud proved this point. . . . When he paid relatively little attention to diagnosis he was optimistic about the amenability of psychoanalysis for a wide variety of patients.

Peter Giovacchini, 1979
p. 60

IN THE INITIAL interviews you must establish whether the patient is indeed one who will be amenable to and benefit from psychotherapy.

Michael Basch, 1980
p. 9

THERE CAN BE no doubt that those individuals whose ability to cope has been demonstrated in the past are far better candidates for any form of psychotherapy than patients whose persistent failures in living are a function of their neurotic problems. . . . The therapist's potential successes are usually commensurate with the available raw material. In this respect, psychotherapy is no different from a medical treatment which may be uniquely effective provided the patient is generally healthy, there are no complications, and the patient is optimally cooperative.

Hans Strupp and Jeffrey Binder, 1984
p. 306

"So ANALYSIS is for the healthy?" "It works better for the healthy. But I haven't seen anything in general medicine where that wasn't the case. The healthier the patient, the better the treatment."

Janet Malcolm, 1981
p. 130

⊒

IN THE INTERVIEW, symptoms are most clearly reflected in what the patient talks about; character traits are revealed in the way he talks and the way he relates to significant other people, particularly to the interviewer. . . . The patient describes his symptoms, whereas his character traits are observed by the doctor.

Roger Mackinnon and Robert Michels, 1971
p. 76

⊒

OFTEN THE patient's symptom represents his identification with an important figure. Hence, it is useful to ask if he has ever known anyone else with similar symptoms.

Roger Mackinnon and Robert Michels, 1971
p. 41

⊒

THE SYMPTOMS or behavior deviations do not necessarily betray the true structure of the ego organization.

Kurt Eissler, 1953
p. 120

Pᴀᴛɪᴇɴᴛs ɪɴ whom currently there is an active, on-going, regressive process, and patients who without previous treatment are consciously aware of thoughts, fantasies or impulses which are ordinarily unconscious, are usually in a position of relative failure of ego defences. . . . Such patients may at times apear to be suitable for intensive uncovering treatment since they seem to have so much "insight," but frequently they lack the other ego capacities to integrate and deal with such insight, and the "insight" proves to be a function of the failing defences.

Paul Dewald, 1964
pp. 118–119

ㄹ

Wɪᴛʜ ᴀɴʏ patient who despairs of life, it is important to find out whether he is or has been suicidal. . . . No matter how the question is phrased, the patient is usually glad finally to be able to discuss the issue with someone, and is reassured that his distress is being taken seriously by the therapist. The exact wording of the question is not important but the manner in which the therapist asks the question is. When asked matter-of-factly, it will usually get an honest answer. If the therapist is embarrassed and ill at ease about the possibility of suicide, the patient may conceal the truth. A statement like, "You're not suicidal, are you?" or "I don't know exactly how to say this, but you haven't—er ah—ever, that is—thought about hurting yourself somehow, have you?" is practically an invitation to the patient not to acknowledge the possible seriousness of his condition; the therapist is clearly not ready to hear about it.

Michael Basch, 1980
pp. 129–130

ㄹ

Tʜᴇ ᴘsʏᴄʜᴏᴛɪᴄ individual, particularly the schizophrenic, has a more basic defect in his capacity for relating to others. This is seen clinically

in his tendency to isolation and withdrawal, with few lasting friend-
ships and a shallowness and superficiality in those that do develop. He
may be less troublesome to get along with than the neurotic, but his
friends and acquaintances will often find him a less stable and less
important part of their lives. . . . The psychotic patient "feels" different; it is harder to make contact with him and to empathize with his
emotional responses.

Roger Mackinnon and Roberts Michels, 1971
p. 77

⊒

ONE HEARS SO much, in the description of patients, about difficulties
in expressing aggression, and so little about difficulty in expressing
love. This latter is really much more important, since the prospects of
cure depend on the capacity for love and not on the capacity for
aggression.

Sidney Tarachow, 1963
p. 103

⊒

IN THE INTERVIEW, the quality of the patient's object relations may
become apparent in his interaction with the interviewer. Although
brief, such diagnostic interactions with patients often permit differentiation of the neurotic personality's gradual build-up of a personal
relation of an appropriate kind from the borderline personality's
persistently chaotic, empty, distorted, or blocked relation.

Otto Kernberg, 1977
p. 106

⊒

. . . COUNTERTRANSFERENCE becomes an important diagnostic tool,
giving information on the degree of regression in the patient and the
predominant emotional position of the patient toward the therapist

and the changes occurring in this position. The more intense and premature the therapist's emotional reaction to the patient, the more threatening it becomes to the therapist's neutrality, and the more it has a quickly changing fluctuating, and chaotic nature—the more we can think the therapist is in the presence of severe regression in the patient. At the other extreme of the continuum, working with patients suffering from symptomatic neuroses and not too severe character disorders, such intensive emotional reactions of the therapist occur only temporarily, after a "build-up" over a period of time (generally past the initial period of treatment), and are of a much less threatening nature in so far as the stability and neutrality of the analyst are concerned.

Otto Kernberg, 1965
pp. 43-44

ᔎ

IT IS THE therapist's inner reaction that is most important in evaluating a patient's situation, especially if there are discrepancies between the communication the patient is trying to make and the reaction he arouses.

Michael Basch, 1980
p. 4

ᔎ

THERE IS ONE practical warning which may serve as an indication that countertransference is in the picture. . . . Beware of the patient who, after the first interview, insists that you are the only analyst for him. Don't think that means you are an especially fine analyst or that you have special ability to understand the patient. It usually means the patient's neurotic defenses are comfortable with you and he anticipates a pleasant symbiosis.

Clara Thompson, 1964
p. 166

MOTIVATION

IT IS NOT a truism that the "better" the motivation, the less the resistance. . . . Since resistance is ubiquitous, the well-motivated patient is not likely to be any poorer in that commodity than the unmotivated one.

Gertrude and Rubin Blanck, 1974
p. 199

⊒

A PATIENT'S statement of willingness to get rid of symptoms is simply a gesture, a price which some professionals like to extract from their patients as a sign of good will.

Ernst Beier, 1966
p. 123

⊒

IT SHOULD NOT be concluded, however, that a patient who appears somewhat unmotivated cannot be educated to become motivated. Patients who appear unsophisticated psychologically can be taught . . . what psychotherapy is all about; after a thorough explanation, a seemingly unmotivated patient may understand what is involved and may become more motivated to understand himself.

Peter Sifneos, 1980
p. 98

⊒

INITIAL IMPRESSIONS

WHEN A PATIENT does not specifically request such a summary, it is best not to give it if the interview has manifestly produced such an understanding in the patient. In such a case, the therapist should suggest only that the pair continue this manifestly productive exploration in further sessions. The nature of the work just concluded will dictate the nature of the work to come.

Sheldon Roth, 1987
p. 87

己

O~NE MUST~ mistrust all prospective patients who want to make a delay before beginning their treatment. Experience shows that when the time agreed upon has arrived they fail to put in an appearance, even though the motive for the delay—i.e., their rationalization of their intention—seems to the uninitiated to be above suspicion.

Sigmund Freud, 1913
p. 125

己

Y~OU MUST NOT~ make interpretations until you have found out what kind of patient it is that you are talking to . And yet, . . you may not be able to find out what kind of patient you are talking to without making interpretations. These two statements are clearly irreconcilable. Is there any way in which they can be reconciled? The simple answer is no, and an obsessional would conclude that the initial assessment interview is therefore impossible.

David Malan, 1979
p. 212

己

TRIAL ANALYSIS

N~O OTHER KIND~ of preliminary examination but this procedure is at our disposal; the most lengthy discussions and questionings in ordinary consultations would offer no substitute.

Sigmund Freud, 1913
p. 124

PATIENT PREPARATION

THE THERAPIST should be as explicit and as clear as possible about the arrangements. . . . Nothing need be implicit or assumed, particularly since changes from the initial arrangements and agreements are more difficult to explore and interpret if there is uncertainty about how these arrangements were originally worked out.

Steven Levy, 1984
p. 14

己

THERE IS ENOUGH that is different, atypical, unexpected, and frightening about therapy without the therapist acting in unexpected ways without explaining why.

Steven Levy, 1984
p. 18

己

IF A PATIENT requests some explanation of what is done in treatment, the best answer comes from merely pointing to the productive interchange that has already taken place, and then suggesting that, in general, more of the same is in the offing. It is a bit like the marketplace philosophy of "what you see is what you get." Such an approach is an early natural precursor of a working alliance built on observable work done, and it minimizes expectations of especially mysterious proceedings that will magically dispel unhappiness.

Sheldon Roth, 1987
pp. 87–88

己

THE FIRST TIME he asks a question I explain why I do not answer it; I am silent the next time.

Ralph Greenson, 1967
p. 215

THE INITIAL INSTRUCTION

G O RIGHT AHEAD speaking and don't feel you have to wait for me to respond or ask questions. If I need to know or want to tell you something, I won't hesitate to interrupt you. Otherwise you go right on with whatever comes to your mind. We'll follow wherever that leads us.

Michael Basch, 1980
p. 22

W E WANT TO learn all we can about you, your background, and how you came to be the kind of person you are. You can tell me about it either by starting from the present and working back or from the past working to the present. I don't know anything about you except what you have told me about yourself and your particular problem. I don't want you to be disturbed about what is pertinent and what is not but simply to say whatever comes to mind without doing any censoring of your own.

Leon Salzman, 1980
p. 273

M Y INITIAL instructions to patients regarding our work in the treatment hours are limited to encouraging them to speak as freely and openly as possible about what goes on in their minds in the sessions, and what is of concern to them in their daily life. Rather than stressing free association in a strict sense, I emphasize full, open communication about what the patient himself thinks is important. The understanding is that I need to know as much as possible about the patient from himself, so I can help him explore those aspects of himself in which his own understanding is limited. After my initial explanations, clarifications, and encouragements to the patients, I then deal with emerging resistances in a standard, interpretive way.

Otto Kernberg, 1975
pp. 194–195

⊒

W HAT THE MATERIAL is with which one starts the treatment is on the whole a matter of indifference—whether it is the patient's life-history or the history of his illness or his recollections of childhood. But in any case the patient must be left to do the talking and must be free to choose at what point he shall begin. We therefore say to him, "Before I can say anything to you I must know a great deal about you; please tell me what you know about yourself."

Sigmund Freud, 1913
p. 134

⊒

. . . I N DIALOGUES with oneself one is more sincere than in conversation with others. The speaker is less inhibited and less conventional and will say what he really thinks, while his audience is more tolerant and more willing to listen, not only to reason, but to unreason. Certainly many matters that are never or rarely mentioned in talking to others are freely discussed in conversations with oneself.

Theodor Reik, 1952
p. 69

⊒

T HE ATTITUDE I wish to inculcate in a patient as early as possible is that talking to me should be like talking to him- or herself.

Sheldon Roth, 1987
p. 80

AN UNWELCOME question which the patient asks the doctor at the outset is: "How long will the treatment take? How much time will you need to relieve me of my trouble?" If one has proposed a trial treatment of a few weeks one can avoid giving a direct answer to this question by promising to make a more reliable pronouncement at the end of the trial period. Our answer is like the answer given by the Philosopher to the Wayfarer in Aesop's fable. When the Wayfarer asked how long a journey lay ahead, the Philosopher merely answered "Walk!" and afterwards explained his apparently unhelpful reply on the ground that he must know the length of the Wayfarer's stride before he could tell how long his journey would take. This expedient helps one over the first difficulties; but the comparison is not a good one, for the neurotic can easily alter his pace and may at times make only very slow progress. In point of fact, the question as to the probable duration of a treatment is almost unanswerable.

Sigmund Freud, 1913
p. 128

EARLY INTERPRETATIONS

TO MAKE EARLY explanations of the content of conflicts is to foster passivity in the patient.

Paul Dewald, 1964
p. 160

. . . THE WAY IN which the therapist responds to the patient's material sets the stage as to whether or not the patient will go on to increasing frankness, or whether he will feel himself to be held responsible for all he says and, therefore, be more cautious and concealing in the material that he produces.

Paul Dewald, 1964
p. 162

Psychoanalytic dialogue . . . is not ordinary conversation, and I believe it is necessary, for the sake of conducting an inquiry in depth, to assume a posture of ignorance vis-à-vis the patient. That is, I assume that I do not understand the reasons or motives behind any of his statements until he explains them to me. At first the patient, until he learns to differentiate the analytic inquiry from ordinary conversation, may experience such apparently naive questions as irritating and react defensively.

Lawrence Epstein, 1982
p. 208

TREATMENT PROMISES

Since the symptom represents unconscious attempt at resolution of an intra-psychic conflict through the construction of a compromise-formation, any promise or assurance that the symptom will be removed unconsciously represents a challenge to the patient's defences. Therefore, such a promise may mobilize anxiety as the patient anticipates facing the unconscious danger situation. . . . To promise a phobic patient that he will be able to go into the phobic situation may mean to the patient that treatment will put him in the very situation of unconscious danger which he is attempting to avoid through his symptom. In this way, unconsciously, the promise of removal of symptoms may actually mobilize further anxiety.

Paul Dewald, 1964
p. 142

On the whole, when the patient-therapist match is good, the patient experiences significant relief in the beginning of treatment.

Sheldon Roth, 1987
p. 162

MANAGEMENT OF EMERGENCIES

Don't ever be upset by emergencies. If you put yourself in the patient's shoes, then all is lost. Patients have a way of re-creating their emergencies. . . . It is bad enough that the patients are frightened by them. At least one of you should not be worried.

Sidney Tarachow, 1963
p. 251

己

Consider the patient's emergency as a chronic problem. The patient will re-create the emergency again tomorrow, to keep his conflict alive, to keep alive the picture either a bad father or a bad mother, or "I am being abused," or "the world is mistreating me," or as atonement for his aggression or what not. He needs it. . . . An emergency is a chronic thing.

Sidney Tarachow, 1963
p. 252

己

The best tack to take is to tell the patient, "Well, you must have done this many times before. This is nothing new to you." The patient will confirm this time after time. The edge of the emergency is lifted and treatment can be more considered and deliberate.

Sidney Tarachow, 1963
p. 252

己

SUICIDE

If there is any reason to suspect suicidal notions or fantasies, it is essential that the analyst insist that the patient spell them out, in as much concrete detail as possible. The explicit statement of all suicidal notions may have a cathartic effect and facilitate reality testing by both patient and therapist.

Leopold Bellak and Peri Faithorn, 1981
p. 172

⊐

FOUR OMINOUS signs of suicide potentiality in depressives are (1) an impatient, agitated attitude that something must be done immediately, (2) a detailed, feasible, lethal suicide plan, (3) pride, suspicion, and hyperindependence as character traits, (4) isolation, withdrawal, living alone, or living with someone so emotionally removed from the suicidal person that the patient, in effect, is living alone.

Robert Litman, 1970a
p. 303

⊐

AS ALWAYS when suicide is in question, the therapist must consider it as a fusion of intense destructive anger expressed self-destructively on the one hand, and love, protectiveness, concern and guilt, on the other—the patient would rather kill himself than harm the other person—and it is usually the anger that needs to be brought into the open.

David Malan, 1979
p. 204

⊐

EVERY ATTEMPTED or completed suicide implies the activation of intense aggression not only within the patient but within his immediate interpersonal field.

Otto Kernberg, 1984
p. 263

THE SUICIDE PLAN

T HIS IS PROBABLY the most significant of the criteria of suicide potentiality. Three main elements should be considered in appraising the suicide plan. These are (1) the lethality of the proposed method, (2) availability of the means, and (3) specificity of the details.

Norman Farberow, Samuel Helig, and Robert Litman, 1970
p. 278

W E DO NOT ask, "How do you plan to do it?" (a question we have heard asked of a patient), because this joins in with the formulation of a suicidal plan which, by himself, the patient might not have developed too far. But one might, if necessary, ask, "Have you gone so far in your desperation that you have thought about what you might do?" The answer to such a question will enlighten the therapist, but the wording is carefully designed to avoid becoming ally to the plan and is meant to indicate that these are desperate, impulsive solutions rather than competent ones.

Gertrude and Rubin Blanck, 1974
p. 266

A T FIRST THE plan seems alien and dangerous to the individual himself and provokes anxiety. Gradually, the suicide plan acquires an autonomous structure within the ego, more or less dissociated from the rest of the self and tolerated as ego-syntonic.

Robert Litman, 1970a
p. 303

SUICIDE ACTIONS occur frequently in alcoholic characters not only because of the ego weakening effects of alcohol, but also because the alcoholic character contains strong self-destructive elements.

Robert Litman, 1970a
p. 302

THE MOST serious suicidal potential is associated with feelings of helplessness and hopelessness, exhaustion and failure, and the feeling, "I just want out." A combination of agitation and confusion, however, particularly in a person who has had a previous psychotic episode, may constitute an emergency. When the predominant feeling is one of frustration, anger, or rage, without overwhelming confusion, the lethal danger is generally somewhat less.

Robert Litman and Norman Farberow, 1970
p. 264

A CRUCIAL POINT in the evaluation is whether the person with a chronic, repetive self-destructive pattern has completely exhausted his emotional resources.

Robert Litman and Norman Farberow, 1970
p. 262

THE PROGNOSIS is most favorable if the patient, although depressed and contemplating suicide, thinks of those who would suffer from his deed. Here, libidinal object cathexis is the ally of life.

Gertrude and Rubin Blanck, 1974
p. 266

SUICIDAL PATIENTS suffer from "tunnel vision" and only see one particular solution. It is therefore important to show them that there are other options.

Leopold Bellak and Peri Faithorn, 1982
p. 173

己

IF THE SUICIDAL trend is severe, the patient should be seen daily. The patient's response to such an optimistic approach may be taken as a rough prognostic guide to the feasibility of office psychotherapy. The outlook is favorable when patients feel relieved after the first interview, with decreased tension and a slight lift in mood, and quickly form a dependent transference relationship to the therapist.

Robert Litman, 1970
p. 406

己

IF THE PSYCHOTHERAPIST reports honest feelings of helplessness in himself and a breaking off of communication between himself and the patient, then it would appear that an emergency situation has developed and it is time for some sort of active intervention.

Robert Litman and Norman Farberow, 1970
p. 265

己

THE POSSIBLE VALUE OF SUICIDAL IDEAS

A SITUATION which seems unbearable at the moment may be felt to be more bearable as long as one has the knowledge that one can get out of it. Thus an idea that one could at any time commit suicide actually has the result of carrying one through an otherwise intolerable experience.

Mary Julian White, 1952
p. 147

As to suicidal preoccupations and fantasies, the word of the German philosopher, Nietzsche, may prove to be helpful while coping with them psychotherapeutically: "The thought of suicide has saved many lives." That is, the knowledge that man is free to end his life if and when its burden becomes unberable has helped many people to cope with their emotional difficulties in living.

Frieda Fromm-Reichmann, 1950
p. 200

TREATMENT OF PREPSYCHOTIC PANIC AND ACTIVE DECOMPENSATION

In the confused, unstable, or fluctuating world of the patient, the therapist establishes himself as a person who emerges as a clear and distinct entity, somebody on whom the patient can sustain himself. The therapist must clarify his identity as an unsophisticated, straightforward, simple person who has no facade to put on, a person who can accept a state of nonunderstanding, a person who has unconditional regard for the dignity of another human being, no matter what is his predicament. An atmosphere of reassurance is at least attempted, and the patient recognizes it. The therapist's appeal at this moment is not to the unconscious of the patient, but to the basic and genuine part of the patient's personality.

Silvano Arieti, 1974
p. 548

The only way you can put a floor under a patient is by getting him to talk about what is most important to him at that moment.

Elvin Semrad, 1980
p. 103

THE MORE disturbed the patient, the more active the therapist must be in helping him *build* (or rebuild) *self-esteem and in helping him structure his life*, at least temporarily, so as to avoid self-esteem-destroying experiences.

Leopold Bellak and Peri Faithorn, 1981
p. 53

WORKING WITH the very disturbed patient, it is important to be aware of the *resources* in the community.

Leopold Bellak and Peri Faithorn, 1981
p. 67

IF CRISES ARISE *in the course of treatment*, it is important to relate them to intercurrent events of external or internal nature. Since the patient is often unaware of the nature of the precipitating event, careful reconstruction of external events in the patient's life is necessary. At the same time, a clear conceptualization of the dynamic events of the preceding therapeutic sessions is necessary. The essential task is *to establish continuity where there is discontinuity* — the basic contribution of psychotherapy.

Leopold Bellak and Peri Faithorn, 1981
p. 43

. . . ONE MUST demonstrate clearly to the patient a continuity between the immediate *panic*, the *precipitating factors* and *life history*. This gives the patient at least some feeling of control over what seems frighteningly ego-alien.

Leopold Bellak and Peri Faithorn, 1981
p. 90

. . . Work of analysis progresses best when the patient's pathogenic experiences belong to the past so that the ego can stand at a distance from them. In conditions of acute crisis it is almost impossible to use analysis. In such states the whole interest of the ego is concentrated on the painful reality, and resists analysis, which seeks to penetrate below the surface and to discover the influences to which the patient has been exposed in the past.

Sigmund Freud, 1937
p. 387

3

How
Therapy
Works

FREUD DISCOVERED that in the end, the main method of helping people to outgrow their buried emotional past and to free themselves for a new development of personality towards friendly, spontaneous, and creative living in the present, was simply to leave the person entirely free to talk out whatever occurred to him. This is not as easy as it sounds, for sooner or later it involves the free voicing of what has for a lifetime been held to be prohibited.

Harry Guntrip, 1971
p. 9

⊒

PSYCHOTHERAPY capitalizes on the half-awareness that life could be more gratifying than it is.

Ernst Beier, 1966
p. 27

⊒

THE YOUNG CHILD tends to externalize his internalized conflicts and then to experience them as a battle between himself and the outside world rather than to see the conflicts as an inner battle. Analysis establishes a consciousness of the inner battle.

Anna Freud, 1980
p. 68

쾨

Initially, as a defence is reduced and the conflict comes closer to consciousness, there will be an increase of anxiety until the material is fully conscious. Once the material is subject to the ego's conscious integrative and controlling processes, there will again be a reduction in the level of anxiety. . . . It is necessary, through lowering of defences, temporarily to mobilize and increase anxiety in amounts that can be tolerated by the patient as part of the process of making unconscious material conscious.

Paul Dewald, 1964
p. 102

쾨

Analysis is an upsetting and "then" a restorative process.

Karl Menninger, 1958
p. 41

쾨

CATHARSIS

It is noteworthy that Freud tried and discarded this method almost a century ago. . . . Any method which fails to include consideration of the ego and its further structuralization will not endure.

Gertrude and Rubin Blanck, 1974
p. 161

... THE TASK OF causal therapy is to correct the pathological emotional patterns formed in childhood. Since these patterns consist of feelings toward other persons, they can only be adequately corrected by working them through as feelings toward one or more other persons. ... The relationship to the analyst is in effect a sample human relationship. The disordered childhood pattern repeats itself in some part and form to the therapist. The task is to work with the mature part of the patient's personality in shared responsibilities, analyzing out the pathological elements, thereby releasing the patient's potential for continuing his natural emotional development.

Leon Saul, 1967
p. 51

TRANSFERENCE

... IN THE REGRESSION induced by the psychoanalytic treatment situation the patient reacts to the analyst in successively different ways: first, as a mysterious medical person who promises some kind of help; second, as a misidentified father, mother, brother, and so forth; third, as a human being with certain weaknesses; and finally, as a human being with certain strengths.

Karl Menninger, 1958
p. 91

... IF A PATIENT'S free associations fail, the stoppage can invariably be removed by an assurance that he is being dominated at the moment by an association which is concerned with the doctor himself or with something connected with him.

Sigmund Freud, 1912a
p. 101

So long as the *patient's communications and ideas run on without any obstruction, the theme of transference should be left untouched.* One must wait until the transference, which is the most delicate of all procedures, has become a resistance.

Sigmund Freud, 1913
p. 139

⊒

Transference, which seems ordained to be the greatest obstacle to psycho-analysis, becomes its most powerful ally, if its presence can be detected each time and explained to the patient.

Sigmund Freud, 1905a
p. 117

⊒

The utmost pressure which we can bring to bear upon the patient in the direction of giving up [the transference] consists in progressively and with ever greater clearness bringing the transference to light which gradually makes it more difficult and a matter of greater conflict for the patient as an adult to play the infantile part that he has to play in the transference.

Franz Alexander, 1925
p. 494

⊒

The problems are relived in an *as if* manner until understood, integrated, and no longer pathogenic.

Sidney Tarachow, 1963
p. 17

RESISTANCE

INSTEAD OF inquiring *how* analysis effects a cure (a point which in my opinion has been sufficiently elucidated) we should ask what are the obstacles which this cure encounters.

Sigmund Freud, 1937
p. 377

THE RESISTANCE accompanies the treatment step by step. Every single association, every act of the person under treatment must reckon with the resistance and represents a compromise between the forces that are striving towards recovery and the opposing ones. . . .

Sigmund Freud, 1912a
p. 103

WE CANNOT evade resistances; he who wishes to operate has to cut and must not be afraid of blood.

Otto Fenichel, 1941
p. 46

WORKING THROUGH

PSYCHOANALYTIC working through is analogous to mastery through play . . . though play indulged in by only part of the ego.

Sidney Tarachow, 1963
p. 17

THE PROCESS OF working-through . . . involves the patient repeatedly extending his awareness of his problems in their different forms and from different points of view, until the desired degree of insight and understanding has been achieved.

Paul Dewald, 1964
p. 244

⊐⊏

MUCH AS WE would like it otherwise, psychotherapy is . . . a long, lumbering process in which the same issues are repeatedly worked through in the therapy environment and are tested and retested in the patient's life environment.

Irvin Yalom, 1980
pp. 307–308

⊐⊏

MUCH TIME IN analysis is spent interpreting the analysand's need to see things as either black or white.

Roy Schafer, 1983
p. 7

⊐⊏

ALTHOUGH FREUD originally applied the concept of "working through" to the laborious and repetitive process of overcoming the patient's resistances to the uncovering process in analysis, more and more ego-oriented analysts have been applying the term to the equally laborious and important task of overcoming the patient's resistances to change, in terms of the achievement of new patterns of thought and behavior. Neither insights, nor confrontations, nor transference interpretations in and of themselves, necessarily produce fundamental change, although occasionally we may be gratified to see change occur only on that basis. More often than not . . . we find it necessary, sooner or later . . . gently and persistently to begin to encourage the patient to come to grips directly with the anxiety-provoking situation, and by a series of graduated successes eventually to achieve the desired sense of mastery.

Judd Marmor, 1979a
pp. 351–352

⊒

. . . INSIGHT alone has no magic qualities.

Paul Dewald, 1964
p. 245

⊒

RECOLLECTION without affect almost invariably produces no result.

Joseph Breuer and Sigmund Freud, 1895
p. 6

⊒

THE THERAPIST must continually operate within the frame of reference that a patient has created his or her own distress. It is *not* chance, or bad luck or bad genes, that has caused a patient to be lonely, isolated, chronically abused, or insomniac. The therapist must determine what role a particular patient plays in his or her own dilemma, and find ways to communicate this insight to the patient.

Irvin Yalom, 1980
p. 231

⊒

UNTIL ONE REALIZES that one has created one's own dysphoria, there can be no motivation to change. If one continues to believe that distress is caused by others, by bad luck, by an unsatisfying job—in short, by something outside oneself—why invest energy in personal change? In the face of such a belief system, the obvious strategy is not therapeutic but activist: to change one's environment.

Irvin Yalom, 1980
p. 231

I'M SHOWING YOU that your own actions defeat your objectives. Why do you take this as criticism, instead of help?

James Masterson, 1983
p. 16

ONE CAN SEE the therapeutic process as one in which the therapist refuses to reinforce the patient's present state of adjustment by re-fusing to make the response the patient forcefully evokes in him.

Ernst Beier, 1966
p. 13

THE THERAPIST who attends to the content of a client's productions as though it itself were the major issue misses the real point of the content: to elicit from and to repeat with the therapist what is dynamically central. . . .

William Mueller and Albert Aniskiewicz, 1986
p. 66

THE UNIQUE contribution of psychoanalysis is the demonstration of the power and persistence of the intrapsychic determinants. But these determinants become only artificial abstractions if they are dealt with in isolation from the interpersonal context in which they find expression.

Merton Gill, 1982
p. 92

⊒

. . . WE MUST TREAT his illness, not as an event of the past, but as a present-day force.

Sigmund Freud, 1914
p. 151

⊒

FOR THERAPY TO proceed, the patient must experience an affect and must see himself or herself in action. . . . Just as a tennis coach cannot correct a student's errors until both can observe them in the course of a game, patient and therapist must become engaged in an interaction before mutative change can occur. First, the patient must act; then, with the help of the therapist, he or she must step back and observe the action; finally, the meaning and purpose of the action must be explored.

Hans Strupp and Jeffrey Binder, 1984
p. 159

⊒

IF, THROUGH CAREFUL examination of the patient–therapist transactions, a particular maladaptive relationship pattern has been articulated, it can be hypothesized with reasonable confidence that the pattern also occurs elsewhere.

Hans Strupp and Jeffrey Binder, 1984
p. 164

I DEMAND, AS best I can by my responses, that she look at what is happening between us rather than just getting angry at me.

Jerome Kroll, 1988
p. 157

回

IF SHE CAN control him with her fury, then he cannot help her face its nature and significance.

Michael Basch, 1980
p. 61

回

HER ABILITY TO become aware of the intensity of the "rescue" motif as she narrated the events in therapy was replaced by her anticipation of the pattern as she caught herself setting up the behaviors themselves. Her self-consciousness of what she was doing ruined the experience for her, and it was no longer available to her.

Jerome Kroll, 1988
p. 147

回

TO "THAW OUT" such "frozen" conflicts between instinct and defense, so that in place of an automatic way of acting a conflict is once more experienced, is indeed a principal task of analysis.

Otto Fenichel, 1941
p. 40

回

WHAT THE THERAPIST no longer permits him [the patient] to do is to use the relationship with a significant person for the purpose of expressing his need in symbolic or disguised ways. The therapist says in effect: "If you want me to coddle you, baby you, protect you, love you, you must experience the feelings associated with these expectations in my presence and as directed toward me. This is predictably painful but it cannot be helped. Once you have undergone this painful experience, you may realize that your expectations were (a) anachronistic—that is, they may have been reasonable in childhood but are no longer useful; (b) unrealistic—that is, as a mature, independent adult I cannot possible coddle you, and, if I did, you would be appalled by it and reject it; or (c) based on gross misperceptions of the current situation as well as that prevailing in your childhood, . . . What I will not allow you to do is to act as if you did not have these expectations of me while at the same time expecting me to fulfill them."

Hans Strupp, 1977
p. 15

⊐

. . . THE VERSION of the patient's life story . . . which constitutes the major source of his or her current unhappiness will be retold to the therapist in may forms and reenacted continually within the therapeutic relationship.

Hans Strupp and Jeffrey Binder, 1984
p. 155

⊐

THE PAST

THE GOOD therapist is the ultimate nostalgia buff; he or she never tires of hearing about the good old days. The past—good, bad but never indifferent—is a storehouse of mood, melancholy, pleasure, and pain—heroes and villains, loves and hates.

Sheldon Roth, 1987
p. 4

How a patient spontaneously represents his past tells us how he needs to see that past *now*. At best his account is only fairly well correlated with the actual past. It is by no means identical with it. The present "autobiography" cannot therefore be taken at face value. Often it is only late in treatment before certain vital corrections are introduced into the patient's initial account of his past. The case history at the beginning and end of treatment may therefore read quite differently.

Roy Schafer, 1954
p. 144

Thus, much recall of the past, . . . is a reconstruction that grows out of present-day needs and interests as well as prejudices and defenses. This is the fallacy of reconstructions of events prior to ages five to six.

Leon Salzman, 1980
p. 282

The therapist should delay reconstructing past traumatic experiences with parents during childhood. Although doing so in order to explain current problems in relationships is often tempting, the patient's profoundly distorted view of the parents and of childhood events, in general, make such interpretations inaccurate and ineffective.

Steven Levy, 1984
pp. 158–159

The psychoanalytic formulation of early experience is difficult and fraught with danger. The reliability of our empathy, a major instrument of psychoanalytic observation, declines the more dissimilar the

observed is to the observer. . . . The early stages of mental development are thus, in particular, a challenge to our ability to empathize
with ourselves, i.e., with our own past mental organizations.

Heinz Kohut, 1971
p. 37

⊐

T HE MOST USEFUL goal of therapy is to provide the patient with a
historically understandable, personal course of events: a coherence
and stability to the patient's experience of self. In treatment, the
therapist strives for comments that have "reconstruction" in mind.
They comprise an assessment of the present in terms of the motiva-
tional building blocks of the past, which in turn provides an organizing framework around the patient's history. Such reconstructions
of how we came to be who we are at the moment will reverberate up
and down the developmental line and show itself in different ways at
different stages of development. The terror of the preadolescent boy
who fears being beaten up by his peers becomes the anxiety of the
college student who fears the jeers and roughhousing of his college
mates.

Sheldon Roth, 1987
p. 154

⊐

I T APPEARS THAT he who cannot recall his past emotional life is not
only alienated from his background but equally estranged from the
present and his contemporary sense of self.

Erwin Singer, 1965
p. 176

⊐

A RE ALL LIFE'S experiences stored in the psyche? Is everything that
cannot be remembered repressed? I prefer to think that some things

are actually forgotten. To use Freud's terms, they either have not been sufficiently cathected (energized), or their cathexes have not been sustained. Consequently, they lose their intrapsychic structure and integration, and simply vanish.

Peter Giovacchini, 1982
p. 5

丩

THOUGH KEENLY interested in how the patient got that way, the therapist is far more interested in why an old trauma, loss, or deprivation continues to exert a powerful influence on the patient's life in the present. The latter influence accounts for the patient's being in therapy.

Hans Strupp and Jeffrey Binder, 1984
p. 167

丩

BOTH PATIENT and therapist must keep in mind that what has happened in earlier life, or childhood, or infancy is not in and of itself crucial in psychotherapy. Rather, it is the ways in which the things that occurred during these phases of a person's earlier development determine, modify or restrict his adjustment in the *current* situations and *current* life experience that is of far greater significance.

Paul Dewald, 1964
p. 171

丩

THE TACTICAL goal of elaboration of earlier life experience is important only if this new understanding of past events and conflicts ultimately results in more effective interaction and adaptation to conflict and stress in the present.

Paul Dewald, 1964
p. 239

WE ARE NOW so used to saying that the causes of neuroses lie back in childhood that we may miss the vital point. . . . It is true that the origins of the trouble were in early childhood, but the actual emotional cause of instability and weakness in the personality in later life is something that is going on in the personality right here and now.

Harry Guntrip, 1969
p. 186

IT MAKES BETTER sense to say that the analyst makes excursions into historical research in order to understand something which is interfering with his present communication with the patient (in the same way that a translator might turn to history to elucidate and obscure text) than to say that he makes contact with the patient in order to gain access to biographical data.

Charles Rycroft, 1966
p. 18

RECONSTRUCTION of the past, in order to make sense of the present, turns into an ongoing process: one, in fact, that proceeds through one's entire life beyond the termination of treatment.

Sheldon Roth, 1987
p. 17

MANY PATTERNS of behavior have been acquired automatically, that is, their rationale has never been examined in the cold light of day.

Hans Strupp and Jeffrey Binder, 1984
p. 191

T HE WHOLE difference between his age then and now works in his favour; and the thing from which his childish ego fled in terror will often seem to his adult and strengthened ego no more than child's play.

Sigmund Freud, 1926
p. 205

⊐

I N TIME, THE patient should be able to recognize his own maneuvers for what they are, as he attempts to cast others, including his therapist, in roles that seem to promise satisfaction of his neurotic needs. Eventually, the anachronistic and unrealistic nature of these needs may dawn upon him. When this happens, the patient faces the bleak disillusionment of realizing that, no matter how imperious they may seem, his infantile needs can never find full gratification in adult role relationships.

Norman Cameron, 1963
p. 227

⊐

A S THIS YOUNG man was enabled to acknowledge all he wanted from me, it rekindled what he wanted from his mother and father (as well as other important figures of his life).

Sheldon Roth, 1987
p. 147

⊐

I T USED TO be one of Winnicott's striking and paradoxical epigrams that the function of the therapist was not to *succeed* but to *fail* . . . . It does not mean that he must fail as a *therapist*, but as a *substitute parent*. The therapist can never make up to his patients for what they have suffered in the past, but what he can do is to repeat the failure to love them enough — which, after all, is intrinsic in the therapeutic situation—and then share with them and help them work through their feelings about his failure.

David Malan, 1979
p. 141

⊒

A ND THE THERAPIST very gently pointed out that what he wanted from him was really no longer available. To this the patient said, "Yes, and I'm very bitter about it."

David Malan, 1979
p. 202

⊒

I T IS WORTH quoting a single moment from this period, when the patient said to his therapist, "I suppose it's inevitable that you become for each of us the very thing that we've wanted all our lives. There must be a lot of disappointed patients around." Thus, without having read the books, he showed a quite remarkable ability to stand back from his therapy, and grasp—no longer with bitterness—its central principle.

David Malan, 1979
p. 206

⊒

T HERAPY IS LIKE life. The initial emphasis is on attachment, developing a loving and dependable bond. Next, there comes an understanding of the pleasures and pains that are part of this bond. All this, however, points in the direction of ultimate loss of parent or the therapist. It is ironic that people seek treatment because of loss of love, fantasied or real, through a process that has loss as part of its inherent structure. Mastery of past pain occurs through mastery of present pain.

Sheldon Roth, 1987
p. 143

Balint CAUTIONS us against having to interpret or in other ways having to act on the feelings the patient elicits; instead, the therapist must "accept," "feel with the patient," "tolerate," "bear with" the patient and the feelings he is struggling with and asking the therapist to recognize.

Thomas Ogden, 1979
pp. 365–366

⊐

Analysis IS NOT only a technical exercise. It is something that we become able to do when we have reached a stage in acquiring a basic technique. What we become able to do enables us to co-operate with the patient in following the *process*, that which in each patient has its own pace and which follows its own course; all the important features of this process derive from the patient and not from ourselves as analysts.

D. W. Winnicott, 1955
p. 16

⊐

. . . In THE PROCESS of psychological healing every person has a certain innate timetable. If the psychotherapist is not aware of each individual patient's unique timetable in the proceedings towards maturity, he may find himself abandoning patients, pressing too hard, and becoming discouraged.

Richard Chessick, 1974
p. 54

⊐

The THERAPIST learns to ride the process rather than to carry the patient.

Edgar Levenson, 1982
p. 13

To A GREAT extent, therapy sets in motion an organic and self-directing process. We oversee this, comment on it, influence some of its momentum, pull and lean against its inertia this way or that, but for the most part, as Freud said, the patient does what "he can or what he wants." In Tolstoi's *War and Peace*, the Russian grand commander, Kutuzov, is considering the question put to him of how he maneuvers hundreds of thousands of soldiers so masterfully. Kutuzov in essence says, "It's rather simple. I look to see in what direction the army is moving, and then I give the order to go in that direction." In many respects, the attentive therapist does the same.

Sheldon Roth, 1987
p. 160

KEEP YOUR agenda out. Remember . . . "You are a servant of the process." The process goes on in her head; your job is to subordinate everything you do to that process.

James Masterson, 1983
p. 33

RATHER THAN starting hours, or summing up hours, or guiding them along, she could acknowledge that the patient was in control, and she could only follow her, not lead her.

Sheldon Roth, 1987
p. 229

IN ALL THERAPEUTIC situations I adhere to one simple and basic principle: so long as the patient is providing some evidence of progress, I leave well enough alone.

Lawrence Epstein, 1982
p. 212

FEELINGS

W E MUST INSIST on talking to patients only about what they actually experience. In other words, go right through the defenses, rather than lose our efforts in helping them strengthen their already strong defenses. The only thing we really deal with in our relationships with patients is their actual life experience—not the stock they came from their heredity, their genes, their biological propensities to growth. All we deal with is their reaction to their life experience; how much of it they integrated and how much of it isn't integrated; how much they can handle and how much they can't handle, but have to postpone or avoid or deny. And the more infantile the personality, the more they handle by avoidance.

Elvin Semrad, 1980
p. 103

⊐

I T IS ALMOST always a relief to experience one's true feelings. . . .

David Malan, 1979
p. 160

⊐

F IRST THEY [feelings] have to be acknowledged, then one has to bear them, and finally one has to decide what to do with them.

Elvin Semrad, 1980
p. 30

⊐

T HE STRONGEST element holding the patient in treatment is your capacity to clarify her feelings on the spot.

James Masterson, 1983
p. 11

W HEN YOU talk about what's important, the patient will always tear.

Elvin Semrad, 1980
p. 140

己

O NCE HE showed his tears, that was enough for me. I respect the autonomic nervous system to show feelings like I respect few other things.

Elvin Semrad, 1980
p. 140

己

P SYCHOTHERAPY with the affect-blocked (that is, feeling-blocked) patient is slow and grinding. Above all, the therapist must persevere. Time after time he will have to inquire, "What do you feel?" "What do you want?" Time after time he will need to explore the source and the nature of the block and of the stifled feelings behind it.

Irvin Yalom, 1980
p. 307

己

A s I WORK, I do not think, "Now, I will be a participant observer." I simply am one. That is, I participate, I respond, I react to my patient and his verbal and non-verbal communications, and at the same time I observe what's going on, what the patient is saying and what he is not saying , evidences of anxiety, what I am feeling and thinking, and where, if anywhere, the interchanges are going, and wondering how best to formulate to the particular patient what I observe.

Ralph Crowley, 1977
p. 357

I LISTEN TO a woman patient. She rambles on and on. She seems unattractive in every sense of the word—physically, intellectually, emotionally. She is irritating. She has many off-putting gestures, She is not talking to me; she is talking in front of me. Yet how can she talk to me if I am not here? My thoughts wander. My head groans. What time is it? How much longer to go? I suddenly rebuke myself. I give my mind a shake. Whenever I think of how much time remains in the hour, I know I am failing my patient. I try then to touch her with my thoughts. I try to understand why I avoid her. What is her world like at this moment? How is she experiencing the hour? How is she experiencing me? I ask her these very questions. I tell her that I have felt distant from her for the last several minutes. Has she felt the same way? We talk about that together and try to figure out why we lost contact with one another. Suddenly we are very close. She is no longer unattractive. I have much compassion for her person, for what she is, for what she might yet be. The clock races; the hour ends too soon.

Irvin Yalom, 1980
p. 415

4

Goals

OUR OBJECT will be not to rub off all the corners of the human psyche so as to produce "normality" according to schedule nor yet to demand that the person who has been "thoroughly analysed" shall never again feel the stirrings of passions in himself or become involved in any mental conflict. The business of analysis is to secure the best possible psychological conditions for the functioning of the ego; when this has been done, analysis has accomplished its task.

Sigmund Freud, 1937
p. 403

. . . ENERGIES THAT were formerly bound to archaic goals are freed and become available to the mature personality.

Heinz Kohut, 1971
p. 31

. . . TO CHANGE the changeable and adjust to the unchangeable.

Thomas Paolino, 1981
p. 178

85

TELLING THE truth about the patient to the patient is the analyst's major task. . . .

Theodore Dorpat, 1977
p. 58

. . . TO HELP THE patient to face the truth about himself, but the analyst must be convinced in himself that this task is not a destructive one.

Ella Freeman Sharpe, 1930
p. 26

. . . TO ENABLE THE patient to separate emotionally from his or her past, to allow the past to sink into obscurity and to lose its influence on the patient's current life.

Richard Chessick, 1980
p. 78

IT IS GENERALLY agreed that influencing the super-ego should be, and in fact is, one of the desirable aims of therapy.

Michael Balint, 1968
p. 4

It HAS OFTEN been said, by myself among others, that the process of recovery consists to a great extent of the patient's putting the analyst (his new father) in the place of the real father who occupies such a predominant place in his super-ego, and his then going on living with the analytic super-ego thus formed. I do not deny that such a process takes place in every case, and I agree that this substitution is capable of producing important therapeutic effects. But I should like to add that it is the business of a real character analysis to do away, at any rate temporarily, with any kind of super-ego, including that of the analyst. The patient should end by ridding himself of any emotional attachment that is independent of his own reason and his own libidinal tendencies. Only a complete dissolution of the super-ego can bring about a radical cure. Successes that consist in the substitution of one super-ego for another must be regarded as transference successes. . . .

Sandor Ferenczi, 1928
p. 98

⊒

The IMPULSE itself need not necessarily become acceptable as a basis for action but must become acceptable as part of oneself.

Erwin Singer, 1965
p. 167

⊒

The GOAL OF analysis is for the patient to become clear about who he is, what he feels and what he wants from others.

Allan Cooper and Earl Witenberg, 1983
p. 259

⊒

One ACHIEVES *mental health to the extent that one becomes aware of one's interpersonal relations*; this is the general statement that is always expressed to the patient. Every one of my patients with whom I have had more than a consultative relationship has received this reply to many different questions, asked throughout the greater part of the work. This is the essential element in replying to the questions, "What ails me?" "How can I get better?" [or] "What good will the treatment accomplish?". . . It is part of the framework that supports all explanations of what is going on, what might be going on, and what will presently be going on.

Harry Stack Sullivan, 1947
p. 207

🔁

[SUPERVISOR]: She does things which alienate people. She doesn't know what she does, she doesn't know how she does it. . . . If she could learn what and how with you, it would be of enormous help. And for her to learn that, you have to be authentic and to be able to share with her what you experience her impact to be. Not irritated, not enraged . . . without hostility. Then she's not being attacked, and that something is being examined, her self-defeating impact. That's a very difficult thing to do because I think we're talking of an analytic growing edge, and something which your patient needs from you . . . which is anxiety laden for you but which you cannot postpone in the service of her therapy.

Leopold Caligor, 1981
p. 20

🔁

THE LISTENING PROCESS becomes more complex as the analyst feels freer to use himself interactively.

Philip Bromberg, 1984
p. 33

🔁

I THINK IT is an excellent technical procedure during uncovering psychotherapy to request patients to bring photographs of the significant people in their lives; I often do this because a photograph fixes better in my mind the person being talked about and brings home to the patient the intensity and the seriousness of my inquiry (as well as providing a mirroring experience).

Richard Chessick, 1980
p. 153

己

. . . IT IS IMPORTANT to have the patient become specific, and not just so the therapist knows what actually happened. The patient's knowledge that he and the therapist have discussed the details of his situation gives the events in question a kind of reality that is qualitatively different from the reality they had when they were vague and private in the patient's mind.

Michael Basch, 1980
p. 25

己

IT IS AN ASTONISHING and hardly noticed psychological fact that one's own words once spoken are differently evaluated than those which we only think in our representations of words.

Theodor Reik, 1952
p. 124

己

. . . ONE HAS INFORMATION about one's experience only to the extent that one has tended to communicate it to another – or thought about it in the manner of communicative speech. Much of that which is ordinarily said to be *repressed* is merely unformulated.

Harry Stack Sullivan, 1947
p. 185

F EW THINGS DO the patient more good . . . than . . . care on the part of the interviewer to discover exactly what is meant. Almost every time one asks, "Well, do you mean so and so?" the patient is a little clearer on what he does mean. And what a relief it is to him to discover that his true meaning is anything but what he at first says, and that he is at long last uncovering some conventional self-deception that he has been pulling on himself for years.

Harry Stack Sullivan, 1954
p. 20

T HUS WHENEVER the psychiatrist's attempt to discover what the patient is talking about leads the patient to be somewhat more clear on what he is thinking about or attempting to communicate or conceal, his grasp on life is to some extent enhanced. And no one has grave difficulties in living if he has a very good grasp on what is happening to him.

Harry Stack Sullivan, 1954
p. 22

K NOWLEDGE OF A life story is acquired in the course of attempting to tell it. . . .

Thomas Schact, Jeffrey Binder, and Hans Strupp, 1984
p. 69

I T IS MY opinion that man is rather staggeringly endowed with adaptive capacities, and I am quite certain that when a person is clear on the situation in which he finds himself, he does one of three things: he decides it is too much for him and leaves it, he handles it satisfactorily, or he calls in adequate help to handle it. And that's all there is to it.

Harry Stack Sullivan, 1954
pp. 22–23

THE *REAL* PROBLEM which I hope finally to uncover, to my patient's satisfaction and with his clear insight, is *what stands in the way of* his making the conventional, and therefore the comparatively simple, adjustment which is regarded as normal. . . . Thus I try to find out why he *can't* do the simplest thing, and in such investigation may come to solve the problem.

Harry Stack Sullivan, 1954
p. 225

DON'T GET SET on curing her, but on understanding her. If you understand, and she understands what you understand, then cure will follow naturally.

Elvin Semrad, 1980
p. 122

ONCE AND FOR all we have to recognize the fact that the first wish of a patient is to be understood. . . .

Michael Balint, 1968
p. 93

W E DO NOT so much want to understand the patient in a purely intellectual vein as we want to appreciate the patient's experience.

Sheldon Roth, 1987
p. 78

⊒

I N ORDER TO help, one has to know a patient differently—emotionally. One cannot truly grasp subtle and complicated feelings of people except by this "emotional knowing." It is "emotional knowing," the experiencing of another's feelings, that is meant by the term empathy.

Ralph Greenson, 1960
p. 418

⊒

W E ARE THEREFORE compelled to begin all over again with the candid question: on what does the so-called born psychologist's keenness in sizing up his object's utterances depend? Essentially on his ability to put himself in the latter's place, to step into his shoes, and to obtain in this way an inside knowledge that is almost first-hand. The . . . name for such a procedure is "empathy." . . .

Robert Fliess, 1942
pp. 212–213

⊒

T HERE SEEMS TO be a tendency among analysts either to take empathy for granted or to underestimate it.

Ralph Greenson, 1960
p. 418

THE CAPACITY to empathize seems dependent on one's ability to modulate the cathexis of one's self-image. The temporary de-cathexis of one's self-image which is necessary for empathy will be readily undertaken only by those who are secure in their sense of identity.

Ralph Greenson, 1960
p. 423

⊐

ONE'S CAPACITY for empathy can be influenced by the other person's resistance or readiness for empathic understanding. There are patients who consciously and unconsciously want to remain ununderstood; they dread being understood. For them to be understood may mean to be destroyed, devoured, unmasked, etc.

Ralph Greenson, 1960
p. 422

⊐

EMPATHY AND intuition are related. Both are special methods of gaining quick and deep understanding. One empathizes to reach feelings; one uses intuition to get ideas. Empathy is to affects and impulses what intuition is to thinking. . . . Empathy is essentially a function of the experiencing ego, whereas intuition comes from the analysing ego.

Ralph Greenson, 1960
p. 423

⊐

. . . ALL METHODS in psychiatry need to be subordinated to this first aim, which is to find where the patient lives. Balint put this as follows: "It happens so rarely in life that you have a person who understands what you are up to and openly faces it with you. That is what we can do for our patients, and that is an enormous thing."

James Gustafson, 1986
p. 118

⊒

T HE AIM IS that the patient should be able to find himself, to accept himself, and to get on with himself, knowing all the time that there is a scar in himself, his basic fault, which cannot be "analysed" out of existence; moreover, he must be allowed to discover *his* way to the world of objects – and not be shown the "right" way by some profound or correct interpretation. . . . It is only to this extent that the analyst should provide a better, more "understanding" environment, but in no other way, in particular not in the form of more care, love, attention, gratification, or protection. Perhaps it ought to be stressed that consideration of this kind may serve as criteria for deciding whether a certain "craving" or "need" should be satisfied, or recognized but left unsatisfied.

Michael Balint, 1968
p. 180

⊒

W ITHIN AN ATMOSPHERE of unconditional acceptance, the therapist establishes a relationship with the patient, the aim of which – usually unspoken – is to enable the patient to understand his true feelings and to bring them to the surface and experience them.

David Malan, 1979
p. 74

⊒

. . . T WO STATEMENTS can be made about the majority of patients whose childhood has been unsatisfactory. First, quite possibly no one – and certainly not the therapist – can make up to them for what they have missed; and second, even if opportunities are offered for some kind of recompense, the patients are in no state to make use of them. . . . They are liable to spoil them in some way. That, of course, is the basic reason why they come for help. It might be thought, therefore, that there is nothing that can be done, but—in many cases at any rate—this is not true. What can be done is . . . their grief and (above all) their anger about past deprivations need to be experienced and worked through. It is then found empirically that they can be brought to the point of accepting those satisfactions that life can offer, even though these may often be nowhere near the recompense that they would like. Put briefly, the aim of therapy is not to make up to patients for the love that they have missed, but to help them work through their feelings about not having it.

David Malan, 1979
p. 141

冒

THE AIM OF giving . . . insight is to enable the patient to face what she (or he) really feels, to realize that it is not as painful or as dangerous as she fears, to work it through in a relationship, and finally to be able to make use of her real feelings in a constructive way, thus changing maladaptive behavior into adaptive behavior.

David Malan, 1979
p. 3

冒

THE ANALYSAND . . . [has] . . . the task of realizing that, while he has the right to expect a modicum of empathic responses from the self-objects of adult life, he must ultimately realize that they cannot make up for the traumatic failures of the self-objects in his childhood.

Heinz Kohut, 1977
p. 260

PATIENTS, HOWEVER, easily miss the real implication . . . as if it were now still a question of relationships with their actual parents. They do not easily grasp the fact that the parents in their dreams are parts of themselves, processes going on in their own minds, and represent now not such much their real parents as their own parent influenced self. . . . It is necessary to make this clear, not only in the interests of solving their internal problems, but also in the interests of allowing for improved realistic relations with the actual parents where they are still alive.

Harry Guntrip, 1969
p. 204

こ

THERAPEUTIC AMBITION

EVERY PATIENT need not be made over: we must not play God.

Sidney Tarachow, 1963
p. 85

こ

[THERAPEUTIC ambition] will not only put him [the analyst] into a state of mind which is unfavourable for his work, but will make him helpless against certain resistances of the patient, whose recovery, as we know, primarily depends upon the interplay of forces in him. The justification for requiring this emotional coldness in the analyst is that it creates the most advantageous conditions for both parties; for the doctor a desirable protection for his own emotional life and for the patient the largest amount of help that we can give him today. A surgeon of earlier times took as his motto the words; *Je le pansai, Dieu le guerit* (I dressed his wounds, God cured him). The analyst should be content with something similar.

Sigmund Freud, 1912b
p. 115

... T HE DOCTOR should hold himself in check, and take the patient's capacities rather than his own desires as guide. Not every neurotic has a high talent for sublimation; one can assume of many of them that they would not have fallen ill at all if they had possessed the art of sublimating their instincts. If we press them unduly towards sublimation and cut them off from the most accessible and convenient instinctual satisfactions, we shall usually make life even harder for them. . . . One must above all be tolerant to the weakness of a patient, and must be content if one has won back some degree of capacity for work and enjoyment for a person even of only moderate worth. Educative ambition is of as little use as therapeutic ambition.

Sigmund Freud, 1912b
p. 119

T HE THERAPIST can do no more than make the possibility of therapeutic relationship available. . . . He has no power, nor should he have, to force the patient to get well against his will.

Harry Guntrip, 1969
p. 338

... T HE ANALYST IS obliged to do his or her best to help create the most favorable conditions for change; the analyst is not obliged to succeed in bringing about change.

Roy Schafer, 1983
p. 156

T HE THERAPIST has to get used to the idea that a session need not be ideal in order to be productive.

Michael Basch, 1980
p. 27

Rather than working toward getting the patient to like him, the therapist needs to work toward being able to like himself as he is functioning with the particular patient in the particular session. (Such an achievement is, incidentally, also the best antidote for negative feelings the therapist may harbor for his patient.) Failure to be satisfied with himself is a clear signal that something is amiss; and, unlike the question of whether the patient cares for him, this area of his behavior as a therapist is one that he can be expected to control.

Michael Basch, 1980
p. 75

⊒

Therapist a: But I'm so afraid of losing her that she is now is control.

Dr. M: . . . you cannot treat anybody under those conditions, i.e., if you are afraid they will leave.

James Masterson, 1983
p. 10

⊒

But what if she does not come back for her next appointment and drops out of treatment? This consideration cannot be a factor in conducting insight psychotherapy. A process geared to helping a patient to face and understand what he has spent a lifetime trying to forget, disavow, or otherwise overlook is not without difficulties. Everyone cannot meet the challenges that inevitably arise as the goal is pursued.

Michael Basch, 1980
p. 62

... THERE IS NO WAY one can ever do a "complete" job in either psychotherapy or psychoanalysis. It is impossible to anticipate everything the patient may encounter in the future and to prepare him for it. All that therapy can do is to help the patient understand himself sufficiently so that when he is faced with the inevitable stresses of life, he does not simply repeat old defensive patterns but, instead, exercises choice in his response based on the present and past significance of the situation at hand.

Michael Basch, 1980
p. 52

PSYCHOTHERAPY is then primarily concerned with preparing the patient for searching and persistent self-investigation and self-awareness by removing those obstacles the patient employs in preventing his becoming his own therapist. . . .

Erwin Singer, 1965
p. 353

THERAPY PROVED of benefit to him by focusing, as effective therapy usually does, on the unexpected.

Irvin Yalom, 1980
p. 372

... IT SEEMS TO me that in psychotherapy especially it is advisable for the physician not to have too fixed a goal. He can scarcely know what is wanted better than do nature and the will-to-live of the sick person. . . . The shoe that fits one person pinches another; there is no recipe for living that suits all cases.

Carl Jung, 1933
p. 60

BRIEF PSYCHOTHERAPY

BRIEF DYNAMIC psychotherapy is rooted in the psychoanalytic tradition. Its fundamental insights and its basic theoretical principles would not have been possible were it not for the ground-breaking discoveries of Sigmund Freud.

Judd Marmor, 1979b
p. 149

⊇

PSYCHOANALYSIS grew out of the cathartic method described by Breuer and Freud in their *Studies on Hysteria*. Many of the elements which today characterize analytically oriented brief psychotherapy can be traced back to that work. Subsequently the development of brief psychotherapy and the development of psychoanalysis were intertwined in such a way that most major attempts at promoting brief psychotherapy were seen by Freud and his followers as attempts to modify and undermine the basic principles of psychoanalysis and thus to destroy psychoanalysis as they understood it.

Walter Flegenheimer, 1982
p. 19

⊇

TO SHORTEN analytic treatment is a justifiable wish, and its fulfillment, as we shall learn, is being attempted along various lines. Unfortunately, it is opposed by a very important factor, namely, the slowness with which deep-going changes in the mind are accomplished.

Sigmund Freud, 1913
p. 130

⊇

CONCERNING the attempts to shorten the time required for psychoanalysis, the cartoon from the *New Yorker* may be cited: A couple is driving fast; the woman says: "And please, no short cuts today; we have no time!"

Otto Fenichel, 1945
p. 573

⊐

Brief therapy can be effective because it is predicated upon very close conceptualization of what ails the patient. The idea is to understand everything, if possible, and then to do only the very little bit that will make a difference. A very old story which demonstrates this point: a general's car broke down and army mechanics were called to fix it. When they were unable to repair the car, they turned for help to an old village smith. The smith took a look at the car, rattled it a little and then banged it sharply. Immediately, the car started up. The general asked, "What do I owe you?" The village smith replied, "A hundred bucks." "A hundred bucks for one bang?" said the general. "No," replied the smith. "One buck for the bang, ninety-nine knowing where to bang." That's the way I see brief emergency psychotherapy. As a modality, I see *brief therapy relating to traditional long-term therapy the way a short story relates to a novel!*

Leopold Bellak, 1980
p. 46

⊐

SELECTION

Short-term dynamic psychotherapy rests on two basic substructures, selection and technique. Each of these is of equal importance. Not all patients are equally suitable for short-term dynamic psychotherapy, but a substantial proportion of those who are ordinarily considered suitable for longer-term analytic procedures are equally suitable for the short-term approach.

Judd Marmor, 1979b
p. 152

T HE UNDERLYING goals of assessment are to identify those patients with the capacity to (1) rapidly enter into a therapeutic alliance, (2) work effectively in an interactional, uncovering treatment, and (3) separate from the therapist once treatment is over with a minimum of distress.

Gregory P. Bauer and Joseph Kobos, 1987
p. 89

ᄅ

M OST OF MY failures in brief therapy have occurred when I have overlooked the patient's inability to provide a "good enough" environment for him- or herself.

James Gustafson, 1986
p. 100

ᄅ

M OST CONTEMPORARY workers in the field agree that short-term dynamic psychotherapy can be used with patients who might be described as relatively "sick" as well as for those with relatively minor problems. Patients with a wide variety of personal disorders and psychoneuroses as well as those with transitional crises may be suitable for short-term dynamic psychotherapy provided they fulfill the selection criteria. The critical issue is not diagnosis so much as the possession of certain personality attributes plus the existence of a focal conflict and a high degree of motivation.

Judd Marmor, 1979b
p. 152

ᄅ

DEVELOPMENT OF A FOCUS

W HAT CLEARLY sets brief psychotherapy apart from long-term psychotherapy is the requirement of working within a focus in the brief technique. A focus is a circumscribed symptom or area of difficulty, the resolution of which will satisfy the present needs of the patient.

Walter Flegenheimer, 1982
p. 5

⊒

Most therapists conducting brief psychotherapy today insist on confining their attention and the goals of therapy to control of the focal issue. This is intended to limit the patient's tendency to regress and thus prolong the therapy.

Samuel Eisenstein, 1980
p. 38

⊒

A focus then becomes a tool for making efficient use of the allotted time.

Thomas Schact, Jeffrey Binder, and Hans Strupp, 1984
p.65

⊒

BEING ACTIVE

In the early 1960s I decided to break away from traditional approach. . . . I began to reverse the tendency toward passivity, becoming more and more active in my technique, yet adhering strictly to three fundamental psychoanalytic principles: releasing hidden feelings by actively working on and interpreting resistance or defenses; paying strict attention to the transference relationship; and actively making links between the transference and significant people in the patient's current life and in the past. . . . As I refined my technique further, particularly by working with the transference relationship, interpreting very actively any manifestation of transference resistance and linking the transference with current relationships and with the past,

I began to realize that the number of sessions required could be reduced.

Habib Davanloo, 1980
p. 45

⊐

THE THERAPIST does not sit back and wait for the material to unfold, but from the very beginning is active in the maintenance of the focus, in the interpretation of the transference, and in the application of the other mechanics essential to time-limited treatment.

Althea Horner, 1985
p. 49

⊐

THIS MORE ACTIVE stance may at times feel somewhat new, different, or foreign to the therapist trained in a more traditional psychodynamic format.

Gregory P. Bauer and Joseph Kobos, 1987
p. 149

⊐

OBVIOUSLY, THIS [activity] does not mean acting out in the analysis, indulging in wild analytic interpretations, or being directive and telling the patient what to do. It does mean actively confronting defenses and resistances, responding empathically to patient distress without forsaking objectivity, and never losing sight of the fact that the goal of analysis is not the interminable exploration of primary process material as an end in itself, but the utilization of all insights toward the focused goal of enabling patients to cope more adaptively with their problems of living.

Judd Marmor, 1979b
pp. 354–355

Like ALMOST every innovation, "activity" on closer inspection is found to be an old acquaintance. Not only has it played an important part already in the early history of psychoanalysis; it has in a certain sense never ceased to exist. We are dealing here, therefore, with the formulation of a conception and of a technical expression for something which, even if unexpressed, has always de facto been in use.

Sandor Ferenczi, 1921
p. 11

⊒

THE TIME LIMIT

When THERAPY must be brief it is best shortened straightforwardly by setting time limits.

Thomas Schacht, Jeffrey Binder, and Hans Strupp, 1984
p. 65

⊒

Both FERENCZI and Rank borrowed from Freud the setting of a time limit to therapy. Freud used it in the analysis of the Wolfman in 1912. . . . This technical parameter was later adopted by Franz Alexander and is employed today by almost all therapists doing brief psychotherapy.

Samuel Eisenstein, 1980
p. 27

⊒

Time LIMITS that are set at the beginning of therapy and of which the patient is recurrently reminded provide a stimulus for serious therapeutic work. The patient realizes that time is at a premium, that he or she should get on with the job, and that the end is always in sight.

Hans Strupp and Jeffrey Binder, 1984
p. 264

It is very probable, too, that the large-scale application of our therapy will compel us to alloy the pure gold of analysis freely with the copper of direct suggestion. . . . But, whatever form this psychotherapy for the people may take, whatever the elements out of which it is compounded, its most effective and most important ingredients will assuredly remain those borrowed from strict and untendentious psychoanalysis.

Sigmund Freud, 1919
pp. 167–168

5

Change
in
Therapy

EXPERIENCE has taught us that psycho-analytic therapy—the liberation of a human being from his neurotic symptoms, inhibitions and abnormalities of character—is a lengthy business.

Sigmund Freud, 1937
p. 373

〓

LET US START from the assumption that what analysis achieves for neurotics is nothing other than what normal people bring about for themselves without its help.

Sigmund Freud, 1937
p. 381

〓

THE THERAPEUTIC successes that occurred under the sway of the positive transference are open to the suspicion of being of a *suggestive* nature. If the negative transference gains the upper hand, they are blown away like chaff before the wind.

Sigmund Freud, 1940
p. 33

IT IS, I THINK, a commonly agreed clinical fact that alterations in a patient under analysis appear almost always to be extremely gradual: we are inclined to suspect sudden and large changes as an indication that suggestive rather than psychoanalytic processes are at work. The gradual nature of the changes brought about in psychoanalysis will be explained if, as I am suggesting, those changes are the result of the summation of an immense number of minute steps, each of which corresponds to a mutative interpretation. And the smallness of each step is in turn imposed by the very nature of the analytic situation.

James Strachey, 1934
p. 144

... IT IS DANGEROUS to let impatience, no matter how nobly motivated, destroy one's realization that personal growth is a solitary and painful and therefore slow process. . . . Speed-up procedures endanger the very heart of *personal* change, individually nurtured and *privately* integrated into the fabric of one's being during agonizing hours of pain. The enormous danger . . . is the horrifying possibility that personal growth will be more apparent that real, resting a good deal on suggestion effects, identification processes (the core of emotional pathology), and unexamined forces making one act in blindness even when the acts performed may seem socially desirable.

Erwin Singer, 1965
p. xiv

CHANGES WHICH are of a long-range nature will have a slower impact on the state of the equilibrium.

Paul Dewald, 1964
p. 18

... Every therapist has made the observation that behavior changes tends to be slow, sometimes excruciatingly so. There is a strong conservative element in human behavior, for the good reason that what one has always done lends security and predictability to one's behavior and that of others.

Hans Strupp and Jeffrey Binder, 1984
p. 191

回

The reason analytic work usually takes years is not because the uncovering process takes that long, but because the process of enabling the patient to generalize the insights achieved in the transference situation and to apply them to the wider arenas of his life does not usually come easily and requires patient, repetitive interpretations of perceptual distortions and defensive rationalizations under an umbrella of benign and consistent emotional support.

Judd Marmor, 1979a
p. 352

回

From the patient's point of view it is very undesirable that psychotherapy ordinarily last a long time. He wishes he could change and be happier as soon as possible. But from the point of view of society, the very fact that "personality" is a relatively stable variable has many desirable consequences. Imagine a society where change could be brought about overnight! We would not only have a very unstable society, but also be subject to the whims and control of manipulators.

Ernst Beier, 1966
p. 8

回

SYMPTOM CURES

The reason symptomatic cures are deemed undesirable lies in the fact that the disappearance of the symptom, no matter how immediately pleasing to all parties concerned, is ultimately a sign that the communicative process has become somewhat reduced, making further explorations more difficult, unless, of course, the disappearance of the symptoms is based upon thorough insight and subsequent resolution of the communicated conflict.

Erwin Singer, 1965
p. 92

SINCE NEUROTICS are persons who in their unconscious instinctual life have either remained on an infantile level or have regressed to it, that is, persons whose sexuality (or aggression) has retained infantile forms, it might perhaps be expected that after the pathogenic defenses are abolished, perverse strivings might come to the fore. Practice shows that there is no such danger. The warded-off portions of instincts have retained their infantile character only because they have been warded off. If the defense is undone, what has been excluded regains connection with the mature personality and fits itself in with if.

Otto Fenichel, 1945
p. 571

BY KEEPING THE feeling–idea complex from again becoming unconscious, the patient has the opportunity to learn how to readjust to the situation in a more adaptive way than he originally did.

Thomas Paolino, 1981
p. 54

IT IS IMPORTANT to keep in mind that the patient will finally have to solve his problems in actual life, in his relationships to his wife and his children, his superiors and his competitors, his friends and his enemies. . . . The sooner the patient can be led against those real obstacles in life from which he retreated and can be induced to engage in new experimentation, the more quickly can satisfactory therapeutic results be achieved.

Franz Alexander, 1946
p 38

An important lesson learned in psychotherapy, particularly in the more intensive variety, is the lesson of human cooperation in achieving mutual goals. On a general level, the patient must gain the experience that if he works constructively with the therapist, the latter will provide constructive help. For example, if the patient works hard at overcoming his inhibitions and secretiveness, the therapist will help him to understand the data and "reward" him through interpretations, clarifications of symbolic meanings, etc. Conversely, the therapist responds with silence and minimal communications to resistive maneuverings. The therapist must learn to gauge his participation in terms of this balance or the patient will fail to appreciate the difference. Since patients have typically learned to dominate powerful adults by negativism, passive-aggressiveness, exploitativeness, etc., as a function of having been dominated, oppressed, and exploited by their parents, the lesson of cooperation and mutuality is one of the most important nonverbal kinds of learning mediated by a skilled therapist. It is amazing how little attention (Erikson being an exception) is paid by major theories to this subtle but powerful function of psychotherapy, and yet it is clearly one of the most important lessons in living that psychotherapy can provide.

Hans Strupp, 1977
pp. 21–22

⊐

... One priceless thing the patient learns in therapy is the limits of relationship. One learns what one can get from other but, perhaps even more important, one learns what one cannot get from others.

Irvin Yalom, 1980
pp. 406–407

⊐

Once we see the world differently, we seem to inhabit a new world.

Arnold Goldberg, 1985
p. 64

. . . ONE COMPREHENDS oneself in order not to be preoccupied with oneself.

Irvin Yalom, 1980
p. 439

⊒

IF HE WANTED to feel better about himself, or even to love himself, he had to stop doing things of which he was ashamed.

Irvin Yalom, 1980
p. 282

⊒

YOU HAVE TO be able to say (feeling and bearing the pang of sadness that goes with it), "I want that, but it's not for me, and I accept it." *Renunciation* is the mechanism of adaptation.

Elvin Semrad, 1980
p. 4

⊒

TO HER REPLY that therapy is not doing enough, I have no soothing answer. Promises of success and exhortatory words of encouragement are . . . [a] pitfall that needs to be avoided here.

Jerome Kroll, 1988
p. 158

SOMETIMES PATIENTS . . . will ask what psychoanalytic therapy will do to their marriage. When clinically indicated, I often respond by saying that a successful therapy will strengthen a healthy marriage and lead to the termination of an unhealthy marriage.

Thomas Paolino, 1981
p. 177

IN . . . CASES where a good result has been obtained after a long treatment, I have always felt that the patient owed as much to those he or she lived with as to me.

Harry Guntrip, 1971
p. 190

THERE ARE MANY environments where a more positive emergence of the patient would be destroyed by the collective action of others who needed him to stay the same for the sake of system stability.

James Gustafson, 1986
p. 87

TERMINATION

. . . THE READINESS to engage in a genuine search and to shoulder its burdens is the hallmark of therapeutic success and therefore the ultimate criterion for termination of therapy. Paradoxical as it may sound, the moment the patient enters therapy fully and genuinely, the therapeutic task has been fulfilled.

Erwin Singer, 1965
p. 353

T HE QUESTION of termination is not, "When is your psychotherapy over?" but "When is it no longer necessary for us to have formal meetings in order that your psychotherapy process may go on in a continuous fashion?"

Richard Chessick, 1974
p. 325

🔁

T OO OFTEN THE mistake is made of thinking that therapy is not over until a better life has become a reality. That leads to an interminable and frustrating kind of situation. Once the patient is ready, like a young adult, he must leave home and take his chances. Therapists no more than parents can prearrange his happiness. . . .

Michael Basch, 1980
p. 104

🔁

SETTING A DATE FOR TERMINATION

T HERE CAN BE only one verdict about the value of this device for putting pressure on the patient. The measure is effective, provided that one hits the right time at which to employ it. . . . The analyst must use his own tact in the matter. A mistake, once made, cannot be rectified. The saying that the lion springs once and once only must hold good here.

Sigmund Freud, 1937
pp. 375–376

🔁

W E DO NOT advocate tampering with the frequency of the sessions — a mechanical and ineffective device. When the patient is ready to terminate, he should do so and not prolong dependency by "tapering."

Gertrude and Rubin Blanck, 1974
pp. 358–359

T ERMINATION evokes memories of earlier separations and the painful affects—grief, rage, devaluation of the love object—associated with the earlier traumas.

Hans Strupp and Jeffrey Binder, 1984
pp. 206–207

⊐

. . . W HILE THE impending termination of the treatment will have the effect of bringing part of the material to light, another part will be walled up, as if buried, behind it and will elude our therapeutic efforts.

Sigmund Freud, 1937
p. 375

⊐

T HE MORE INTENSE the patient's transference reaction has been during the course of the therapy, and the greater the degree of regression in the service of the ego, the more intense will be the experience of loss and grief, and therefore the need for mourning and grief-work. The more that the patient during treatment has avoided the development of a transference relationship, and the more that the transference has been denatured or weak, the less intense will be the experience of loss and the accompanying grief. . . . The patient's resolution of his conflicts will also be less effective and meaningful.

Paul Dewald, 1964
p. 275

⊐

I N THE ANALYSIS of the transference neuroses, the terminal phase is frequently characterized by a return to structural conflicts that had been the major content of the working through carried out during the main part (the "middle phase") of the analysis. Once more, it seems, as the necessity for the ultimate severance of oedipal ties is now at hand— as the imminent final parting from the analyst confronts the patient with the ultimate relinquishment of the objects of his childhood love and hate—once more does the child in him try to assert the old demands before it finally decides to set them aside for good or succeeds indeed in dismissing them.

Heinz Kohut, 1977
p. 15

NOT INFREQUENTLY there is a persistence of the fantasy of ultimate gratification in the transference up to the time that the termination is announced and planned. Dynamically, the termination of treatment may have the unconscious significance to the patient of ultimate frustration of transference wishes. . . . In as much as the termination may represent ultimate frustration of transference gratification, and there is less fantasied gain from maintaining the defences against its expression, there is likely to be an intensified mobilization of negative transference in the termination phase. If this negative transference can be successfully resolved during the termination phase, there may occur a more rapid maturation on the basis of conscious acceptance of the frustration of drive-derivatives.

Paul Dewald, 1964
pp. 273–274

ANOTHER FREQUENT resistance is the verbalization of feelings of disappointment in the therapy, and feelings that little or nothing of significance has been accomplished. This frequently represents an attempt to emphasize that the loss is not a significant one, and thereby to avoid the experience of grief.

Paul Dewald, 1964
pp. 279–280

Not infrequently the decision that the treatment has not been successful may be a mutual one between the therapist and the patient. . . . At times it may be indicated for the therapist to offer his help in arranging for subsequent treatment with someone else. However, if there are significant negative transference factors in the current treatment failure, these may be displaced to the next therapist if he is chosen by the present one.

Paul Dewald, 1964
p. 272

As I was finally leaving Fairbairn after the last session, I suddenly realized that in all that long period we had never once shaken hands, and he was letting me leave without that friendly gesture. I put out my hand and at once he took it, and I suddenly saw a few tears trickle down his face. *I saw the warm heart of this man with a fine mind and a shy nature.*

Harry Guntrip, 1975
p. 149

It would be folly to believe that psychotherapy will activate the patient's total capacity to love and care and to use his powers fully and productively. All that one may hope for is that he will become engaged in a never-ending effort to love, to care, and to use his abilities fully and creatively. Belief in the perfectibility of man is not synonymous with belief in a perfect man.

Erwin Singer, 1965
p. 353

LET US PAUSE for a moment to assure the analyst that he has our sincere sympathy in the very exacting requirements of his practice. It almost looks as if analysis were the third of those "impossible" professions in which one can be sure only of unsatisfying results. The other two, as has long been agreed, are the bringing-up of children and the government of nations.

Sigmund Freud, 1937
p. 401

6

Attachment

AT NO TIME from his first psychoanalytic writings to his last did Freud ever lose sight of or minimize the importance of the affective relationship between patient and analyst. Throughout his work on the process of treatment a kind of running battle may be detected between the respective claims of understanding and attachment, although when one looks more closely one sees that it is not equal combat, but a struggle for survival on the part of understanding. To be sure, Freud was very much the champion of the voice of reason, but while he was cheering it on, he seemed to be advising his friends not to bet on it.

Lawrence Friedman, 1978
p. 526

⊒

IT REMAINS THE first aim of the treatment to attach him to it and to the person of the doctor. To ensure this, nothing need be done but to give him time. If one exhibits a serious interest in him, carefully clears away the resistances that crop up at the beginning and avoids making certain mistakes, he will of himself form such an attachment and link

119

the doctor up with one of the imagos of the people by whom he was accustomed to be treated with affection.

Sigmund Freud, 1913
p. 139

⊒

T HE THERAPIST must become a trusted ally in the patient's quest for relief from his problems, someone the patient will come to know a good deal about in terms of the therapist's way of understanding mental life.

Steven Levy, 1984
p. 126

⊒

POSITIVE TRANSFERENCE

[I T] IS THE STRONGEST motive of the analysand for co-operating in the work of analysis.

Sigmund Freud, 1937
p. 388

⊒

H OW DO YOU motivate people to get back into the world? By letting them fall in love with you. How else?

Elvin Semrad, 1980
p. 120

⊒

W ITHOUT TRANSFERENCE love the patient would have insufficient motivation to endure the unhappiness of analytic investigation.

Sheldon Roth, 1987
p. 150

T HUS THE SOLUTION . . . is that transference to the doctor is suitable for resistance to the treatment only in so far as it is a negative transference or a positive transference of repressed erotic impulses. If we "remove" the transference by making it conscious, we are detaching only these two components of the emotional act from the person of the doctor; the other component, which is admissible to consciousness and unobjectionable, persists and is the vehicle of success in psychoanalysis exactly as it is in other methods of treatment.

Sigmund Freud, 1912a
p. 105

. . . T HE INTERPERSONAL relationship between patient and therapist continually oscillates between the valid adult–adult relationship of the present and the anachronistic child–parent relationship of the past.

Hans Strupp and Jeffrey Binder, 1984
p. 35

I BELIEVE THAT it is neither correct nor useful to distinguish between transference and therapeutic or working alliance.

Charles Brenner, 1979
p. 137

J UST AS THE pre-Freudian physician was ineffective partly because he remained a fully "real" person, so the psycho-analyst may be ineffective if he remains a fully "symbolic" object. The analytic situation requires the therapist to function as both, and the patient to perceive to him as both. Without these conditions, "analysis" cannot take place.

Thomas Szasz, 1963
p. 442

... THE THERAPIST may designedly enter all the phenomenology of the patient as a real object. This may be permitted to occur in some aspects of the treatment of psychoses, notably schizophrenia, and in the treatment of the young and certain acting-out psychopaths.

Sidney Tarachow, 1963
p. 10

FACILITATING THE COLLABORATION

... I WANT TO GIVE him whatever educational means he needs in order to help him become an analytic patient; to help him work in the analysis. I do not want to make him an analyst, but I want him to be familiar with certain aspects of the process of being analyzed after he has experienced them, so that he can cooperate with me to the best of his conscious ability.

Ralph Greenson, 1967
p. 125

WE CANNOT REPEATEDLY demean a patient by imposing rules and regulations upon him without explanation and then expect him to work with us an adult. . . . For a working alliance it is imperative that the analyst show consistent concern for the rights of the patient throughout the course of the analysis. This means that we indicate our concern not only for the neurotic misery the patient brought into the analysis and suffers outside of the analysis, but also for the pain that the analytic situation imposes on him.

Ralph Greenson, 1967
p. 214

CLEARLY IN THE proper therapeutic atmosphere the patient and the therapist work together as partners in an effort to understand and accept or reject various constructions and interpretations as hypotheses. The patient must participate actively in this; therefore, when resistances arise these must be attended to first.

Richard Chessick, 1980
p. 185

⊐

COLLABORATION does not develop when left entirely in the hands of the patient. The most willing of patients soon loses interest in trying to communicate with a Great Stone Face who overdoses the session with silence.

Kenneth Colby, 1958
p. 19

⊐

USUALLY THE sex of the therapist does not matter. . . . We see no reason to begin a case under a handicap, however, if the patient has strong feelings about it

Gertrude and Rubin Blanck, 1974
p. 182

⊐

. . . THE THERAPIST cannot usefully demand higher regard than the patient's level of object relations permits.

Gertrude and Rubin Blanck, 1974
p. 353

COLLABORATION is . . . not prematurely imposed on all patients. For may patients, especially those presenting primitive mental states, authentic collaboration will be possible only if preceded by a long series of mutative interpersonal interactions . . .

Lawrence Epstein, 1982
p. 195

⊒

IT IS ALSO useful to bear in mind that the therapeutic alliance, at its best, is not reciprocal. . . . [It] fluctuates markedly, if not wildly, on the patient's side, despite the widely held belief that there can be a steadfast ego which remains constant in the treatment.

Gertrude and Rubin Blanck, 1974
p 199

⊒

I WISH TO suggest that the patient can only appreciate in the analyst what he himself is capable of feeling.

D. W. Winnicott, 1949
p. 70

⊒

TERMS LIKE "therapeutic alliance," "working alliance," or "therapeutic contract" have often come to imply a mutuality of goals between patient and therapist that is unrealistic to anticipate and that should not be expected as the basis for treatment. . . . In practice these terms are often used to mean that the therapist must get the patient to like him and must, in turn, like the patient. Psychotherapy is not a popularity contest. A patient's fear of intimacy, the expectation of being hurt, and other reasons may cause him to behave antagonistically toward his therapist and to present himself so as to be unlikable. I believe that the therapist is mistaken if he makes his primary goal the establishment of "rapport." (Nor, by the way, is he guaranteed easy sailing by immediate mutual appreciation and admiration between himself and a patient; such feelings can be as much defensive and countertherapeutic as their antitheses.)

Michael Basch, 1980
pp. 74–75

⊒

THE IMPORTANCE OF ATTACHMENT

SHE TOOK NO medication at all on those mornings [of therapy], and would arrive feeling pretty ill, but always by the end of the session felt much better and found that a "person" was better than a "pill," a highly important discovery for her, for she had been under heavy medication for years.

Harry Guntrip, 1969
p. 338

⊒

ALTHOUGH, AS A rule, it is not stated quite so explicitly, we are compelled to recognize that the two most important factors in psychoanalytic therapy are interpretations and object relationship. It should be born in mind, however that with the latter we are on comparatively unsafe grounds because psychoanalytic theory knows much less about it.

Michael Balint, 1968
p. 159

⊒

FAIRBAIRN POINTED out that deep insight only develops inside a good therapeutic relationship. That is because the patient cannot stand it if he feels alone.

Harry Guntrip, 1969
p. 353

W E REQUIRE THE patient to abandon his infantile objects, and offer adult objects in exchange. *Without this incentive perhaps no treatment of any kind would be possible.* This could be a principle in education, too. After all, education is basically tolerance of pain and abandonment of pleasure. We cannot offer renunciation alone—we must also offer an object, generally the teacher.

Sidney Tarachow, 1963
p. 21

I N CLASSIC OEDIPAL analyses the importance of a therapeutic relationship is not absent. It is merely not so conspicuous because the patient's need for it is not as great. With schizoid, borderline, and some psychotic patients, this need can emerge with imperative force and dominate the treatment, and it is only its emergence and acceptance by the therapist that makes a good result possible.

Harry Guntrip, 1971
p. 188

"H UMAN ATTACHMENT" has to be given to us as infants, if we are to be able to become secure as adults. Moreover, those who do not have this experience as part of their basic personality make-up are excessively vulnerable even to the slightest risk of loss of support. Their chronic over-dependency is a genuine compulsion that they cannot, by effort or will-power, not feel. Their only hope is to find someone who can understand this and help them to grow out of it. This is what psychotherapy is.

Harry Guntrip, 1971
p. 118

FROM THE THERAPEUTIC viewpoint . . . one must first fuse in order to separate.

Sheldon Roth, 1987
p. 122

⊒

DEPENDENCY problems are not necessarily worked through by the use of words which denote dependency.

Ernst Beier, 1966
p. 89

⊒

. . . A NUANCE OF the analyst's attitude can determine the difference between a lonely vacuum and a controlled but warm human situation.

Leo Stone, 1951
p. 21

⊒

[THE PATIENT'S] problem is that he must risk dropping all pretences with himself that he is more adult and tough than he really feels to be deep down, in order that he may come back to the anxious child that he once was and still feels to be inside; and begin again from there, and this time in the security of a parental personal relationship, to treat this injured part of himself in a more constructive manner that promotes genuine growth instead of an artificial toughness as a mask for hidden fear.

Harry Guntrip, 1969
p. 206

Iт sᴇᴇᴍs тнᴀт only if patients are allowed to "regress"—that is, to give up the security gained by relying on the "caretaker" services of their false ego—which means that only if their analyst can take over the "caretaking" by "managing the regression," can an atmosphere be created in which interpretations can reach, and then become intelligible and acceptable to the real ego.

Michael Balint, 1968
p. 111

⊒

SYMPATHETIC UNDERSTANDING
OF THE PATIENT

I ɢʀᴀɴт, ᴏF course, that the analyst must be ready to listen with human sympathy to his patient's story of his difficulties and that he must give them his complete attention and apply all his knowledge. The "sympathetic understanding" is not, [however] as you might expect . . . present from the start of the work. It is one of its optimal results. It comes toward the end of the treatment or emerges when the analysis has already progressed considerably. One may compare its development with the reading of a really great novel. You do not love its figures immediately or it would not be a work of art. It takes time and some psychological work on you part to penetrate to the essence of the personalities you are reading about, to learn what makes them tick and what the motives are that determine their actions and feelings. . . . The more he discovers of those emotional undercurrents, the deeper he goes into the domain of unconscious processes, the more his patient becomes "sympathetic" to him, the more "reconciled" he becomes to him. At the end he cannot help but see in him a human being like himself, struggling with the same conflicts that are common to us all, proud and humble, almost ready to give up but somehow going on—down but not out. At the end the analyst realizes that there no longer exists a gulf between him and his patient. . . . Sympathetic understanding does not mark the beginning of analysis, but its end.

Theodor Reik, 1952
pp. 129–130

7

Transference

IN THIS WAY the transference took me unawares, and, because of the unknown quantity in me which reminded Dora of Herr K., she took her revenge on me as she wanted to take her revenge on him, and deserted me as she believed herself to have been deceived and deserted by him.

Sigmund Freud, 1905a
p. 119

[SUPERVISOR]: . . . I cast about quickly for a point at which to seize the situation, particularly for the provocation for this impulse to murder. I could not think of anything until I reminded myself of the best working rule in psychotherapy or in psychoanalysis. Where should one look if anything arises that one does not understand?

Resident: To the transference.

Sidney Tarachow, 1963
p. 295

⊐

I HAVE BEEN thanked during analytic hours for successful business transactions, for winning a law suit, for conquering a beloved woman,

for making a technical discovery, for good luck at poker — all achieve-
ments of which I was wholly innocent. But I have also been accused of
causing the outbreak of World Wars I and II, losses on the New York
Stock Exchange, an attack of measles in a child a thousand miles way,
defeat in a tennis game, the loss of a husband or wife — all happenings
of which I was equally innocent. I have been blessed and cursed a
thousand times, killed and kissed in thought, annihilated and royally
rewarded in fantasy, and all because I sit unseen in a chair behind a
woman or a man and listen to what he thinks or feels — simply because
I am an analyst. So powerful is fantasy working in broad daylight.

Theodor Reik, 1952
p. 111

⊐

T HE IMPACT OF these highly charged emotions brings about a curious
inequality in the relationship between analyst and patient. The
analyst is felt as a powerful, vitally important person, but only so far as
he is able or willing to gratify, or to frustrate, his patient's expectations, hopes, desires, and needs; beyond this sphere the analyst, as an
everyday, real person, hardly exists. Of course, the patient has all sorts
of fantasies about his analyst but these, as a rule, have more to do with
the patient's inner world than with the analyst's real life and real
personality. Although in comparison with the analyst the patient
usually experiences himself as weak and far less important, it is only he
(the patient) who matters, and matters enormously; it is exclusively his
wishes, urges, and needs that must be attended to, and it is his
interests that must be the focus of attention all the time.

Michael Balint, 1964
pp. 84–85

⊐

W HAT ARE TRANSFERENCES? They are the new editions or facsimiles of
the tendencies and phantasies which are aroused and made conscious
during the progress of the analysis; but they have this peculiarity,

which is characteristic of their species, that they replace some earlier person by the person of the physician. To put it another way: a whole series of psychological experiences is revived, not as belonging to the past, but as applying to the person of the physician at the present moment.

Sigmund Freud, 1905a
p. 116

⊐

THE CHILD INTERNALIZES the parents through their attitudes and treatment of him and also by identification with them. The parents form *imagos* in the child's mind; they are *introjected* as parts of the child's superego. The child takes over in its mind the parents' attitudes, feelings, and behavior to it; and the child continues to react to these imagos as he did to his parents. Further, he projects these imagos onto other persons, and therefore reacts to these other persons in some part as he did to his parents.

Leon Saul, 1967
p. 43

⊐

IT CANNOT BE disputed that controlling the phenomena of transference presents the psycho-analyst with the greatest difficulties. But it should not be forgotten that it is precisely they that do us the inestimable service of making the patient's hidden and forgotten erotic impulses immediate and manifest. For when all is said and done, it is impossible to destroy anyone *in absentia* or *in effigie*.

Sigmund Freud, 1912a
p. 108

⊐

INSTEAD OF HAVING to deal as best we may with conflicts of the remote past, which are concerned with dead circumstances and mummified personalities, and whose outcome is already determined, we find ourselves involved in an actual and immediate situation, in which we and the patient are the principal characters and the development of which is to some extent at least under our control.

James Strachey, 1934
p. 132

⊡

P SYCHOANALYTIC "observation" is concerned neither with what has happened nor with what is going to happen but with what "is" happening.

W. R. Bion, 1967
p. 272

⊡

M OREOVER, THE relation of transference brings with it . . . further advantages. If the patient puts the analyst in the place of his father (or mother), he is also giving him the power which his super-ego exercises over his ego, since his parents were, as we know, the origin of his super-ego. The new super-ego now has an opportunity for a sort of *after-education* of the neurotic; it can correct mistakes for which his parents were responsible in educating him.

Sigmund Freud, 1940
p. 175

⊡

ITS DISCOVERY

T HIS CONCEPT [transference] is the corner-stone of psycho-analytic method as well as theory, and was created through the delicate collaboration of three people — Anna O., Breuer, and Freud. Anna O. possessed the relevant basic facts; Breuer transformed them into usable scientific *observations*, first by responding to them in a personal way, and second by reporting them to Freud; Freud was the *observer* and *theoretician*.

Thomas Szasz, 1963
p. 440

THE FACT THAT Anna O. was not Freud's patient has, I think, not received the attention it deserves. Possibly, this was no lucky accident, but a necessary condition for the discovery of the basic insights of psychoanalysis. In other words, the sort of triangular situation which existed between Anna O., Breuer, and Freud may have been indispensable for effecting the original break-through for dealing scientifically with certain kinds of highly charged emotional materials; once this obstacle was hurdled, the outside observer could be dispensed with.

Thomas Szasz, 1963
p. 440

IN EVERYDAY LIFE, too, there are transference situations. It is a general human trait to interpret one's experiences in the light of the past. The more that repressed impulses seek expression in derivatives, the more hampered is the correct evaluation of the differences between the present and the past, and the greater is the transference component of a person's behavior.

Otto Fenichel, 1945
p. 30

IF A CAPACITY for transference did not exist, the original family sources of love would be irreplaceable. . . . Adaptation has provided humans with a certain degree of flexibility to combat the reality of the family's inability to satisfy all of a family member's needs.

Sheldon Roth, 1987
p. 18

RESISTANCE TO TRANSFERENCE

IT MAY HAPPEN that a patient will not be particularly concerned with his analyst for a short period of time, because important events are going on in his life apart from the analysis. However, prolonged absence of feelings, thoughts, or fantasies about the analyst is a transference phenomenon, a transference resistance. The analyst is too important a person in the life of the analysand to be absent from his thoughts and feelings for any considerable period of time. If the analyst is really not important, then the patient is not "in analysis."

Ralph Greenson, 1967
p. 158

⊒

. . . PATIENTS TEND TO avoid recognizing that they experience and react to the therapeutic relationship in any way other than an uncomplicated professional fashion.

Hans Strupp and Jeffrey Binder, 1984
p. 186

⊒

. . . [FREUD] REACHED the interesting conclusion that the patient's resistance to recognizing transference feelings is equally as great as the resistance to acknowledging conflictful feelings towards the external object of the infantile environment.

Peter Giovacchini, 1982
p. 78

⊒

ADVANCES IN UNDERSTANDING TRANSFERENCE

WE ARE MORE sensitive too to the ways in which the patient may attempt to manipulate or provoke the analyst to react in a particular way, attempting to *make him behave* in the present in the way in which the patient's infantile objects were seen (or fantasied) to behave in the past.

Joseph Sandler, Alex Holder, Marie Kawenoka,
Hanna Engl Kennedy, and Lily Neurath, 1969
p. 634

己

EVERY PATIENT HAS special skills, developed to involve another person, to constrict this other person's response activity, and to maintain in this manner his present state of adjustment.

Ernst Beier, 1966
p. 35

己

WITHOUT EVER having been closely examined, . . assumptions have been carried forward automatically from earlier phases of the patient's life. The assumptions . . . persist because patients unwittingly and self-defeatingly orchestrate significant relationships so as to evoke reactions from others that confirm their fears and anticipations.

Hans Strupp and Jeffrey Binder, 1984
p. 137

己

WHAT THE PATIENT has learned (or thinks he has learned) about human nature in contacts with significant figures during his formative years reveals itself in his attitudes and his conscious and unconscious reactions to the therapist.

Erwin Singer, 1965
p. 265

F URTHERMORE, the patient will unconsciously seek to draw from the therapist behaviors that reenact the role assigned to the object in the patient's enduring scenario. . . .

Hans Strupp and Jeffrey Binder, 1984
p. 35

Ⴒ

T HE PLAY DOES not change; only the actors do.

Michael Basch, 1980
p. 117

Ⴒ

. . . T HE UNCONSCIOUS transference forces are far more significant than are the conscious ones, and in fact they frequently determine the nature of the latter.

Paul Dewald, 1964
p. 260

Ⴒ

A LL TRANSFERENCE phenomena are ambivalent because the nature of the object relationship which is transferred is more or less infantile and all infantile object relations are ambivalent.

Ralph Greenson, 1967
p. 229

... A CONSISTENT POSITIVE or negative transference is a myth.

Gertrude and Rubin Blanck, 1974
p. 149

THE DIFFERENCE, as Sullivan saw it, between a psychotic and neurotic transference was that in the psychotic almost all of the behavior was transference, and there was very little sense of current reality.

Clara Thompson, 1952
p. 105

... THE MORE REGRESSED the individual, the greater can the distortions be in the transfer of feelings from past objects on to the therapist.

Paul Dewald, 1964
p. 194

THE MORE DEEPLY disturbed the patient is, the more decidedly he has abandoned his ability to experience and grasp his own nature and the nature of others correctly, and the more trying his transference reactions will be.

Erwin Singer, 1965
p. 267

. . . [TRANSFERENCE] is based on rigid proclivities to interpret events in a certain way without the flexibility to consider alternatives.

Hans Strupp and Jeffrey Binder, 1984
p. 137

THE ESSENCE OF the analytic process is the formation of transference as the patient allows himself to regress.

Peter Giovacchini, 1979
p. 469

THIS STRUGGLE between the doctor and the patient, between intellect and instinctual life, between understanding and seeking to act, is played out almost exclusively in the phenomena of transference. It is on that field that the victory must be won—the victory whose expression is the permanent cure of the neurosis.

Sigmund Freud, 1912a
p. 108

. . . WE MAY SAY that the patient does not *remember* anything of what he has forgotten and repressed, but *acts* it out. He reproduces it not as a memory but as an action; he *repeats* it, without, of course, knowing that he is repeating it.

Sigmund Freud, 1914
p. 150

T HE MAIN INSTRUMENT, however, for curbing the patient's compulsion to repeat and for turning it into a motive for remembering lies in the handling of the transference. We render the compulsion harmless, and indeed useful, by giving it the right to assert itself in a definite field.

Sigmund Freud, 1914
p. 154

T HE PHYSICIAN . . . must get him to re-experience portions of his forgotten life, but must see to it, on the other hand, that the patient retains some degree of aloofness, which will enable him, in spite of everything, to recognize that what appears to be reality is in fact only a reflection of the past.

Sigmund Freud, 1920
p. 19

. . . T HE PATIENT'S developing relationship with the therapist acts like a magnet which attracts to it attitudes and feelings, both positive and negative, pertaining to earlier love objects in the patient's life.

Hans Strupp and Jeffrey Binder, 1984
p. 156

RESIDENT: I wonder if anyone has experimented with a paranoid patient by bringing his hated object to him, and having this presumed hating object show obvious signs of affection. What might happen?

Supervisor: In a psychoanalysis the transference is used to carry out almost precisely the experiment you are suggesting. The patient converts the analyst into the hated and hating object, and it is up to the analyst to call the patient's attention to the distortions which the patient is imposing on the figure of the analyst.

Sidney Tarachow, 1963
p. 289

目

T HE THERAPEUTIC effort is to try to get a grasp of the manner in which the patient re-creates his problem with you in the transference. . . . You stay with the patient until you become important to him, and when you are important you play out some role that has been assigned you.

Sidney Tarachow, 1963
p. 253

目

I N AN ANALYSIS the analyst must treat everything as transference, particularly emotional outbursts at him. What saves the analyst's composure is his grasp of the fact that the outburst is a transference phenomenon. The moment he gets involved in reality the way the patient does, his therapeutic potential as an analyst is ruined. The patient hates you and you start hating him and that is the end of therapy. This is the analytic base line.

Sidney Tarachow, 1963
pp. 294–295

目

W HAT SAVES THE therapeutic situation is the therapist's knowledge of and self-confidence in the transference. If you show that confidence, the patient will realize it too, and he too will then begin to treat his rages as rage at someone else.

Sidney Tarachow, 1963
p. 295

O<small>N THE OTHER</small> hand, not everything is transference that is experienced by a patient in the form of affects and impulses during the course of an analytic treatment. If the analysis appears to make no progress, the patient has in my opinion the right to be angry, and his anger need not be a transference from childhood—or rather we will not succeed in demonstrating the transference component in it. . . .

Otto Fenichel, 1941
p. 95

⊒

W<small>HO SHALL SAY</small> now which is "reality" and which "transference"? The point is that the analyst does not find the patient's reactions pre-labelled, as it were; on the contrary, he must do the labelling himself.

Thomas Szasz, 1963
p. 433

⊒

THE DEVELOPMENT OF TRANSFERENCE

T<small>HE MORE OFTEN</small> the sessions are scheduled, and the longer the treatment is expected to last, the more intense transference reactions tend to be and the more useful they become in the therapeutic uncovering and resolution of unresolved unconscious conflict.

Steven Levy, 1984
p. 100

⊒

THE ANXIETY INVOLVED IN TRANSFERENCE ANALYSIS

. . . W<small>ORK WITH THE</small> transference is that aspect of analysis which involves both analyst and patient in the most affect-laden and potentially disturbing interactions. Both participants in the analytic situation are motivated to avoid these interactions.

Merton Gill, 1979
p. 266

⊒

IT IS SAFE to say that at no stage of an analysis are the analyst's reactions, or his convictions about the fundamental truths of psychoanalysis, put to a more severe test than during that stage when the ground of the patient's conflict has been shifted, from external situations or internal mal-adaptations of a symptomatic sort, to the analytic situation itself.

Edward Glover, 1955
p. 108

⊒

. . . FAINT-HEARTEDNESS in making transference-interpretations is responsible for more stagnation in analysis than any other attitude.

Edward Glover, 1955
p. 177

⊒

NEGATIVE TRANSFERENCE

IN MY EXPERIENCE . . . the insufficiently analyzed negative transference is the most frequent cause of stalemated analysis.

Ralph Greenson, 1967
p. 233

⊒

IN SO FAR AS negative attitudes toward the analyst are not analyzed or even expressed, the need of the patient to be reassured of the love and protection of the analyst becomes enormously increased and demanding.

Phyllis Greenacre, 1954
p. 678

⊒

Hostility AND anger early in the analysis, before a reliable working alliance is established, tempt the patient to act out and break off the analysis. The early negative transference must therefore be pursued vigorously, in order to forestall such a development. One can afford to be more passive in working on the positive transference. However, once a working alliance has been established, the emergence of the negative transference can be an important sign of progress. The reliving of hostility and hatred to the early childhood figures in the transference is a most productive phase of the analytic work as long as a good working alliance is present.

Ralph Greenson, 1967
p. 235

⊒

Analyzing THE negative transference does not always mean asking an angry patient, "Why are you angry with me?" but often rather inquiring, "Why do you not dare to show that you have feelings of anger against me?"

Otto Fenichel, 1941
p. 95

⊒

THE EROTIC COMPONENT

If SOMEONE'S need for love is not entirely satisfied by reality, he is bound to approach every new person whom he meets with libidinal anticipatory ideas.

Sigmund Freud, 1912a
p. 100

THERE IS ONLY one thing for the analyst to say to the patient who has fallen in love with him—in one way or another—and that is "Tell me more about it. Say whatever comes into your mind about it. Let's go into it deeper. Let's learn about the nature of you love."

Janet Malcolm, 1981
p. 149

LET'S TRY TO understand what has been happening, let's try to understand why you love and how you love. What do you find lovable about me?

Ralph Greenson, 1967
p. 228

FREUD EVENTUALLY recognized that when the patient, in the transference, falls in love with the therapist, it is the therapist, and no one else, the patient loves.

Steven Levy, 1984
p. 96

EROTICIZED transferences that develop rapidly in initial stages of treatment and reveal a smoky aura of sexuality and seductiveness are usually a sign of the degree to which early maternal issues will be cardinal in the future development of the transference neurosis.

Patients who display such transferences despair of forming adequate and safe trusting relationships except with sexuality as the bonding force.

Sheldon Roth, 1987
p. 36

T O TRANSFER . . . is to generalize in relatively unquestioning terms. To do this requires a more or less prominent disregard of the therapist as he actually is, pressing him into a mold no matter how much it violates his reality. To distort another person by ascribing angelic qualities is by no means less disrespectful than to invest him with diabolic tendencies. In either case his personality is disregarded and attacked.

Erwin Singer, 1965
pp. 276–277

RESOLUTION OF TRANSFERENCE

T RANSFERENCE analysis is the slow and painful experience of clearing the ground of left-overs from past experience, both in transference and counter-transference, so that therapist and patient can at last meet "mentally face to face" and know that they know each other as two human beings. This is without doubt the most important kind of relationship of which human beings are capable and it is not to be confused with erotic "falling in love."

Harry Guntrip, 1969
p. 353

T HE ULTIMATE rescuer is seen in the full light of day as only another person after all.

Irvin Yalom, 1980
p. 407

8

Resistance

IT IS A LONG superseded idea, and one derived from superficial appearances, that the patient suffers from a sort of ignorance, and that if one removes this ignorance by giving him information (about the causal connection of his illness with his life, about his experiences in childhood, and so on) he is bound to recover. The pathological factor is not his ignorance in itself, but the root of this ignorance in his inner resistances; it was they that first called this ignorance into being, and they still maintain it now. The task of the treatment lies in combating these resistances. Informing the patient of what he does not know because he repressed it is only one of the necessary preliminaries to the treatment. If knowledge about the unconscious were as important for the patient as people inexperienced in psychoanalysis imagine, listening to lectures or reading books would be enough to cure him. Such measures, however, have as much influence on the symptoms of nervous illness as a distribution of menu-cards in a time of famine has upon hunger.

Sigmund Freud, 1910
p. 225

THE ANALYSIS IS created by a continuing examination and interpretation of its progress and the obstacles to its further progress.

Roy Schafer, 1983
p. 21

冱

THE OVERCOMING of resistances is the part of our work that requires the most time and the greatest trouble. It is worth while, however, for it brings about an advantageous alteration of the ego which will be maintained independently of the outcome of the transference and will hold good in life.

Sigmund Freud, 1940
p. 179

冱

SINCE RESISTANCE is a manifestation of the defensive and distorting function of the ego, it is resistance which psychoanalytic technique attempts to analyze first. Insight can be effective only if the patient is able to establish and maintain a reasonable ego. Resistances interfere with the reasonable ego and have to be analyzed before any other analytic work can be done with success.

Ralph Greenson, 1967
p. 27

冱

NO ONE WHO is familiar with the nature of neurosis will be astonished to hear that even a man who is very well able to carry out an analysis on other people can behave like any other mortal and be capable of producing the most intense resistances as soon as he himself becomes the object of analytic investigation.

Sigmund Freud, 1913
p. 126

THE PURPOSE OF RESISTANCE

... THERE ARE ALSO aspects of ego function which oppose the process of therapy ... although the patient wishes relief from his neurotic suffering and disability, he does not want to give up the neurosis itself since it represents his attempt to solve a psychological conflict, and as such represents the best level of adaptation he has been able to achieve on his own.

Paul Dewald, 1964
p. 96

⊐

THIS CLINGING TO the closed inner world seems based on the fear that, since one must have parents at all costs, bad parents are better than none, and if you break away you will be out of the frying pan into the fire. That attachment is also at work is shown in the patient who operated all his parents' standards against himself even though he disagreed with them. There is deep loyalty to the parental mores. The antilibidinal ego goes on "bringing the patient up" in the same way as the parents did.

Harry Guntrip, 1969
p. 203

⊐

THE PROCESS OF maturation and the giving up of the neurosis mean that the patient must accept the frustration of his infantile wishes, and must give up the infantile pleasure principle in favour of the reality principle. Unconsciously, the patient clings to the hope of gratification of these drives, and hence he is further resistant to efforts at helping him to find substitute but more reality-oriented satisfactions.

Paul Dewald, 1964
p. 97

ALL THROUGH treatment, the patient is constantly discovering that he has what feel to him more important purposes to serve than getting over his illness or solving his personality problems. He may still feel determined to revenge himself on his family, or by transference, on the therapist. In that case he will use the analysis to get worse . . . in that a negative therapeutic reaction enables him to expose the bad parent or even the whole bad family, and the bad analyst all in one.

Harry Guntrip, 1969
p. 338

己

THE NEGATIVE THERAPEUTIC REACTION

[IT] HAS BEEN described by Freud as the most serious obstacle to psychotherapy. . . . It is the bad object that is predominantly responsible for this reaction—the treacherous road upon which the therapeutic process often flounders. The patient and therapist enduring the travails of the therapeutic journey often resemble Odysseus and his crew forced to outwit the demons, sirens, witches, and cyclops threatening to thwart the long voyage. In fact, those mythological demons personify the manifold masks of the bad object often described as exciting (but not satisfying), enticing, bewitching, addicting, engulfing, rejecting, punishing, and persecuting.

Jeffrey Seinfeld, 1990
p. ix

己

THE BAD OBJECT is comprised of the actual negative attributes of the parental figures—often a composite of the features of both mother and father along with later significant others resembling them—and the child's fantasies and distortions about these figures.

Jeffrey Seinfeld, 1990
p. ix

Therapeutic progress threatens the patient and the therapist with the terrible wrath of the bad object. The patient is conflicted between his loyalty and fear of the bad object and the longing to enter into a good object relationship that will promote separation from the bad object. It is the threat of loss that releases the bad object from repression, resulting in the negative therapeutic reaction.

Jeffrey Seinfeld, 1990
p. x

The therapeutic value of the negative therapeutic reaction derives from considering the bad object transference as a recapitulation of the early developmental vicissitudes of the bad object. The therapeutic approach to the bad object transference is one that combines empathic response with interpretive intervention.

Jeffrey Seinfeld, 1990
p. 303

In the evolution of psychotherapeutic thinking resistance has come to be . . . viewed by many . . . as an expression of the patient's conviction that he has found some way, no matter how painful otherwise, to minimize anxiety and maintain some semblance of self-esteem, dignity, and life. . . . [It] reflects both the patient's disbelief in an alternative way of life . . . his desperate holding on to familiar self-esteem-furthering operations and at the same time his intense fear that any other approach to living would be self-esteem-shattering.

Erwin Singer, 1965
p. 235

However severe the suffering they consciously experience, the analyst must assume that it is less than what they unconsciously anticipate they would feel were they to "get well."

Roy Schafer, 1985
p. 70

I will often comment of the character defenses that they were adaptive at one time and are an indication of the person's determination to survive. This recognition enhances the self-esteem which is bruised by the awareness of the pathology of the self.

Althea Horner, 1980
p. 195

. . . What is neurotic about resistance is the patient's implied inability to appreciate the fact that the valid premises for survival of yesteryear are not necessarily valid today.

Erwin Singer, 1965
p. 233

In my opinion, there is a confusion . . . between the concepts of resistance and defense. I would argue that defense is an intrapsychic concept while resistance is an interpersonal one.

Merton Gill, 1982
p. 37

Resistances represent the continuing operation and function of the patient's ego defenses as they emerge and are manifest in the thera- peutic situation.

Paul Dewald, 1964
p. 221

⊒

The patient should be told at an appropriate time that the detection of resistance and the analysis of resistance are important, worthy, and respectable parts of psychoanalysis. Resistance is not an error or a fault or a weakness of the patient. He is not to feel criticized or rejected for having resistances.

Ralph Greenson, 1967
p. 124

⊒

A patient broke through prolonged periods of compulsive silence by asking the psychiatrist questions about his personal life. The therapist did not fall into the trap of interpreting this as an expression of the patient's curiosity engendered by her attachment to him. He understood that the same anxiety which had kept the patient silent so far was now operating in her verbalizations. Therefore, his response to the patient's questions about him was to the effect that, should she remain interested, he would have no objections to answering these questions at some later date. For the time being, however, he was more interested in and therefore wished to instigate the patient's interest in the reasons prompting her to replace therapeutic curiosity about herself with concern about the doctor's personal affairs. After that the psychiatrist could demonstrate to her that the anxiety she felt in dealing with him, which she tried to ward off at all costs, was the reason for her remaining silent or talking about him instead of discussing her problems.

Frieda Fromm-Reichmann, 1950
p. 108

DOES THE THERAPIST refrain from answering the question and instead ask for association? Not if he feels that the patient cannot tolerate the delay and will react to his request for further associations with structural regression and acting out. Does the therapist respond first and then ask for associations? That may be preferable at this specific point with this particular patient, because the therapist will minimize frustration and maximize the possibility that the patient will feel willing and able to explore his question further.

Andrew Druck, 1989
p. xi

THE PATIENT WILL ask questions. Freud has said that the patient's questions should always be answered by himself. This is a golden rule, but it has its exceptions. We learn to sift these questions.

Ella Freeman Sharpe, 1930
p. 31

THE PATIENT'S curiosity about the therapist, although it will inevitably be frustrated as part of the therapeutic procedure, should not be frustrated with the idea of making it go away or of giving it a pejorative meaning. Rather, it should become part of the material to be learned from, provided the reason for the frustration has been explained so that neither the patient nor the therapist continues to feel in the dark or surprised about the way the frustration was handled.

Steven Levy, 1984
p. 19

THE MOST CONSISTENT way of maintaining the analytic attitude is to approach what traditionally has been called resisting in an affirmative manner, that is, to approach it not as resisting or opposing but as puzzling or unintelligible behavior that requires understanding.

Roy Schafer, 1983
p. 168

... R<small>ATHER THAN</small> setting oneself to "break through resistances," one should try to elucidate their role in the life that is being studied, and, one hopes, beneficially modified in the analysis.

Roy Schafer, 1983
p. 75

I<small>N INVITING THE</small> patient to examine a resistance, the therapist is implicitly challenging a rigid mode of relatedness. Since patients (unconsciously) dare not relinquish habitual patterns that serve to maintain some form of interpersonal security, it is expected that they will often intensify defensive efforts (dig in) or substitute others that serve the same purpose.

Hans Strupp and Jeffrey Binder, 1984
p. 186

T<small>HE MARK OF</small> the professional psychotherapist, in contrast to the novice, is the capacity to recognize silent defenses and resistances at work in the therapy and the willingness to have it out with the patient in regard to these vital defensive systems, even at the risk of incurring great anger on the part of the patient and spoiling the pleasant atmosphere in which the patient, on the surface, seems to be intellectually cooperative.

Richard Chessick, 1980
p. 182

. . . Whenever analysands are confronting their resistant strategies, they will, as a rule, bring up analogous problems and impasses in their past and present extra-analytic relationships. Their difficulties in being and remaining analysands are at bottom no different from their difficulties in all their relationships, including their relationship with, or attitudes toward, themselves.

Roy Schafer, 1983
p. 79

⊐

One must allow the patient time to become more conversant with this resistance with which he has now become acquainted, to work through it, to overcome it. . . .

Sigmund Freud, 1914
p. 155

⊐

The patient's ability to recognize a resistance will depend on two things: the state of his reasonable ego and the vividness of the resistance.

Ralph Greenson, 1967
p. 104

⊐

Making the unconscious conscious is helpful only if doing so alters the dynamics of a neurotic conflict. There is no point in uncovering the repressed if it will meet the same defensive forces which caused it to be repressed in the first place. A change must first be made in the resisting agency.

Ralph Greenson, 1967
p. 137

. . . O<small>NE SHOULD ALWAYS</small> take up the defense before taking up that which is being defended against.

Roy Schafer, 1983
p. 75

⊒

I<small>NTERPRETATIONS</small> around early negative transference manifestations are extremely important. . . . Comments like "it is all right to be angry with me" often backfire because they attempt to bypass rather than explore the patient's difficulties with such negative feelings.

Steven Levy, 1984
p. 98

⊒

S<small>UPPOSE THE</small> analysand is evidently struggling not to cry: Why the struggle? The analyst interested in resistant strategies will first want to know the answer to this question, for that answer will do more for the analysis than the crying itself. . . . The crying, if it is genuine, will take place in good time . . .

Roy Schafer, 1983
p. 75

⊒

W<small>HAT I ADVOCATE</small> you do is try to convey to the patient not a sense of curiosity about what was omitted, but a sense of interest in the meaning of the omission, Commonly, he will simply tell you what was omitted and ignore your why-question; at such times you can continue with, "I didn't mean to ask you what it was you left out, or simply draw your attention to the fact that you left it out; rather, I'm trying to explore the reason you left it out, the meaning of your having omitted it from your deliberations."

I. H. Paul, 1978
p. 136

W HEN A PATIENT becomes silent, the . . . therapist, instead of asking, "What are you thinking?" may ask "What stopped you from talking?"

Thomas Paolino, 1981
p. 196

⧉

I F THE THERAPIST interrupts the silence, it is not to introduce a new topic, but rather to focus on the meaning of the silence itself.

Roger Mackinnon and Robert Michels, 1971
p. 101

⧉

THE ANALYSIS OF RESISTANCE

[I T] DOESN'T MEAN that you shake your finger at the patient and say, "*You're resisting!*" That's the worst thing you can do. . . . The right way is just to point out to the patient how he keeps himself from thinking certain things and feeling certain things, so that he becomes self-conscious and the evasion doesn't work so automatically. That's all. That's the analyst's scalpel. He can't open up his patient's mind and reach in and start tinkering. The only thing he can do is tell the patient, "Look there," and most of the time the patient doesn't look. But sometimes he does, and then his automatic behavior becomes less automatic.

Janet Malcolm, 1981
pp. 72–73

⧉

A S A FOCUS in therapy, the resistance becomes as important as the material that is resisted. In the resistances, we find the elements of conflict embedded in character. Thus, with the obstinate patients, we slowly begin to observe with them that, rather regularly, they tend to say "no" before they ever say "yes." This first . . . is made without interpretation, without suggesting that we understand anything beyond what we observe. Indeed, we can go no farther until the patient consistently makes a similar observation.

Sidney Tarachow, 1963
p. 132

⊒

FREUD HAD always emphasized that in the clinical situation what is most important and relevant is not *what* a patient hides but *how* he hides it.

M. Masud R. Khan, 1969
p. 392

⊒

IN ORDER TO analyze resistance . . . one must take many narrations presented by analysands in terms of *can* and *can't* and retell them in terms of *do* and *don't* and sometimes *will* and *won't*.

Roy Schafer, 1983
p. 232

⊒

THE QUESTION, "Why is the patient resisting?" can be reduced to: what painful affect is he trying to avoid.

Ralph Greenson, 1967
p. 127

⊒

THE USE OF SELF-DISCLOSURE TO OVERCOME
RESISTANCE

IT MIGHT BE expected that it would be quite allowable and indeed useful, with a view to overcoming the patient's existing resistances, for the doctor to afford him a glimpse of his own mental defects and conflicts and, by giving him intimate information about his own life, enable him to put himself on an equal footing. One confidence deserves another, and anyone who demands intimacy from someone else must be prepared to give it in return. . . . Experience does not speak in favour of an affective technique of this kind. Nor is it hard to see that it involves a departure from psycho-analytic principles and verges upon treatment by suggestion. It may induce the patient to bring forward sooner and with less difficulty things he already knows but would otherwise have kept back for a time through conventional resistances. But this technique achieves nothing towards the uncovering of what is unconscious to the patient. It makes him even more incapable of overcoming his deeper resistances.

Sigmund Freud, 1912b
pp. 117–118

W HAT MEANS have we at our disposal for overcoming this continual resistance? Few, but they include almost all those by which one man can ordinarily exert a psychical influence on another. In the first place, we must reflect that a psychical resistance, especially one that has been in force for a long time, can only be resolved slowly and by degrees, and we must wait patiently. In the next place, we may reckon on the intellectual interest which the patient begins to feel after working for a short time. But lastly–and this remains the strongest lever–we must endeavour, after we have discovered the motives for his defence, to deprive them of their value or even to replace them by more powerful ones. . . . One works to the best of one's power, as an elucidator (where ignorance has given rise to fear), as a teacher, as the representative of a freer or superior view of the world, as a father confessor who gives absolution, as it were, by a continuance of his sympathy and respect after the confession has been made.

Sigmund Freud, 1895
p. 282

T HERE IS SADNESS and mourning in letting go of traits that one has
carried for virtually a lifetime; they are old friends.

Sheldon Roth, 1987
p. 149

9

Interpretation

INTERPRETATION is defined as explaining or giving a meaning. When the patient is explaining himself to us and/or to himself without impediment, there is no need for us to speak. We interpret when we believe that we have come to understand something about the patient that he or she cannot fathom or organize without our help.

Michael Basch, 1985
p. 33

⊐

THE SUPPLY OF interpretations, like that of advice, greatly exceeds the need for them.

Harry Stack Sullivan, 1947
p. 92

⊐

[IT] MAY BE likened to a valuable drug which has to be used sparingly if it is not to lose its efficacy.

Wilhelm Reich, 1949
p. 37

Above all, one must be sparing with interpretations, for one of the most important rules of analysis is to do no unnecessary talking; over-keenness in making interpretations is one of the infantile diseases of the analyst.

Sandor Ferenczi, 1928
p. 96

⊒

An interpretation should rarely go as far as possible. It should, by preference, fall short even of its immediate intended goal. This gives the patient an opportunity to extend your interpretation, gives him a greater share in the proceedings, and will mitigate to some extent the trauma of being the victim of your help. . . .

Sidney Tarachow, 1963
p. 49

⊒

. . . One must be careful not to give a patient the solution of a symptom or the translation of a wish until he is already so close to it that he has only one short step more to make in order to get hold of the explanation for himself.

Sigmund Freud, 1913
p. 140

⊒

The psychiatrist should never feel as if he were a clever detective outwitting the culprit in a simple maneuver. Instead, he should make a point of instigating the patient's interest in cleverly discovering for himself the hidden meaning of his intricate communications.

Frieda Fromm-Reichmann, 1950
p. 127

ANY INTERPRETATION which a patient is able to unearth for himself is more impressive to him, hence more likely to produce an immediate and lasting curative effect, than any interpretation offered by the therapist.

Frieda Fromm-Reichmann, 1950
p. 128

⊒

IN PSYCHOTHERAPY, where the patient is being seen at much longer intervals than in psychoanalysis, it is . . . important for the psycho-therapist to be more active than the analyst needs to be, and to be ready to take more chances on making interpretations.

Michael Basch, 1980
p. 42

⊒

STYLE OF INTERPRETATION

NOTHING IS MORE harmful to the analysis than a school-masterish, or even an authoritative, attitude on the physician's part. Anything we say to the patient should be put to him in the form of a tentative suggestion and not of a confidently held opinion, not only to avoid irritating him, but because there is always the possibility that we may be mistaken. It is an old commercial custom to put "E. & O.E." ("errors and omissions excepted") at the bottom of every calculation, and every analytic statement should be put forward with the same qualification.

Sandor Ferenczi, 1928
p. 94

⊒

THE STYLE OF interpretation we prefer is that it be made tentatively and in question form whenever possible. Thus one avoids appearing omniscient, and even saves face sometimes when a decidedly definite interpretation turns out to be an incorrect one . Interpretations that begin, "Don't you think that . . ." or "Isn't it possible that . . ." give the patient room to think, to disagree, or to correct and amend interpretations that may fall short of the mark. Providing an opportunity to participate in the interpretive process also constitutes an ego "stretching" device.

Gertrude and Rubin Blanck, 1974
p. 318

⊒

ONE MIGHT SAY that in the end the interpretations must be seen as co-authored.

Roy Schafer, 1983
p. 109

⊒

I DON'T LIKE this term "point out," because it implies that you've made up your mind and he has to take it. I would rather ask, ask, ask, and let him give you the data. Use the data you get to present to him and further ask. Present your conclusions to the patient as observations on which he can comment. People don't value anything except what they make for themselves.

Elvin Semrad, 1980
p. 118

⊒

TECHNICAL SKILL in analysis is as much dependent on an ability to propose useful questions as on formulating penetrating interpretations. A sagacious, freshly angled question from the analyst opens up new ways for the patient to look at himself and can excite a curiosity to search previously unconsidered possibilities.

Kenneth Colby, 1958
p. 22

ASKING "WHY"

THE PATIENT USUALLY does not know why he became sick at this time or in this particular way, or even why he feels as he does . The doctor wants to learn "Why?" but in order to do so he must find ways to encourage the patient to reveal more about himself. Whenever "why" comes to the doctor's mind, he could ask the patient to elaborate or provide more details.

Roger Mackinnon and Robert Michels, 1971
p. 19

◫

. . . QUESTIONS beginning with the word "why" are likely to arouse the same defensive emotional reactions parents aroused when they "ask" a child, "Why did you do that?" "Why do you feel that?" These are rhetorical questions which communicate disapproval. The patient rarely gets past hearing the disapproval and reacting defensively to it, with no gain in information about himself.

Ralph Crowley, 1977
p. 356

◫

THERAPIST: I HAVE noticed, and wonder if you have. . . .

Steven Levy, 1984
p. 76

◫

TIMING

THE THERAPIST'S understanding may constitute a correct interpretation *for the therapist*, but may not be at all well-timed for the patient.

Thomas Ogden, 1979
p. 367

Topics that produce more psychic pain than mental traffic can bear can be returned to at a more opportune moment.

Sheldon Roth, 1987
p. 80

⊒

In some analyses—though by no means in all—the analyst will even have to realize that a patient whose childhood self-object had failed traumatically in this area will require long periods of "only" understanding before . . . dynamic-genetic explanations given by the analyst—can be usefully and acceptably taken.

Heinz Kohut, 1977
p. 88

⊒

Gentle questioning . . . produced great resistance, and it was considered best judgment to allow the man to regulate his own internal psychic traffic and to assume he was more in touch with what it could bear than I was.

Sheldon Roth, 1987
p. 37

⊒

It is not difficult for a skilled analyst to read the patient's secret wishes plainly between the lines of his complaints and the story of his illness; but what a measure of self-complacency and thoughtlessness must be possessed by anyone who can, on the shortest acquaintance, inform a stranger who is entirely ignorant of all the tenets of analysis that he is attached to his mother by incestuous ties, that he harbours wishes for the death of his wife whom he appears to love, that he conceals an intention of betraying his superior, and so on! I have heard that there are analysts who plume themselves upon these kinds of lightning diagnoses and "express" treatments, but I must warn everyone against following such examples. Behaviour of this sort will completely discredit oneself and the treatment in the patient's eyes and will arouse the most violent opposition in him, whether one's guess has been true or not; indeed, the truer the guess the more violent will be the resistance. As a rule the therapeutic effect will be nil; but the deterring of the patient from analysis will be final.

Sigmund Freud, 1913
p. 140

리

I T IS NOT within the capacity of psycho-analysis entirely to spare the patient pain; indeed, one of the chief gains from psycho-analysis is the capacity to bear pain. But its tactless infliction by the analyst would only give the patient the unconsciously deeply desired opportunity of withdrawing himself from his influence.

Sandor Ferenczi, 1928
p. 90

리

I T IS ONE OF the most important characteristics of a therapist that he should be able to sense the degree of rapport existing at any given moment in a therapeutic session. Anyone who has this capacity can set it up as a kind of thermometer between him and the patient, and can use the moment-to-moment fluctuations in the level of rapport in order to gauge the appropriateness of what he has just said.

David Malan, 1979
p. 20

리

B EFORE MAKING an unwelcome interpretation, therefore, the therapist must estimate whether the patient's trust and confidence in him is sufficient to stand the strain.

Thomas French, 1946
p. 138

THE PATIENT, HOWEVER, only makes use of the instruction in so far as he is induced to do so by the transference; and it is for this reason that our first communication should be withheld until a strong transference has been established.

Sigmund Freud, 1913
p. 144

の

INTERPRETATIONS EARLY IN THERAPY

[T HEY] ARE A VERY powerful tool, and—like powerful drugs—have major side effects, not all of them desirable in an initial interview. They may cause increased disturbance, raise strong hopes that help will be available, or produce immediately a strong attachment to the interviewer. *The one thing we must not do is to produce these side effects and then leave the patient high and dry.*

David Malan, 1979
p. 212

の

INTERPRETATIONS are more effective if they are specific.

Roger Mackinnon and Robert Michels, 1971
p. 37

の

SO IT PAYS, unless there is clear reason for being a bit subtle and obscure, to be quite simply direct and clear. In your personal experience you have no doubt encountered people whose minds leap in such a fashion from topic to topic that every second thing they say astonishes you. With time and enough peace of mind you might figure out how various remarks arose out of what was being said or what had been asked, but by and large you merely have the feeling: "Well, that's a queer kind of person."

Harry Stack Sullivan, 1954
p. 209

ⅎ

Do NOT ENGAGE in far-fetched constructions. Learn to feel comfortable in acknowledging that you are at a loss. It can be a powerful lesson in reality testing.

Hans Strupp and Jeffrey Binder, 1984
p. 47

ⅎ

When AN interpretation has no effect, one often asks oneself: "How could I have interpreted more deeply?" But often the question should more correctly be put: "How could I have interpreted more superficially?" . . . Deep conflicts also have their representatives in the trifles of everyday life, and it is there that the patient can really become aware of their effectiveness.

Otto Fenichel, 1941
p. 44

ⅎ

. . . What is ULTIMATELY of significance for the analytic process is not what the analyst says, or thinks he says, but what the patient experiences in connection with what the analyst says.

Paul and Anna Ornstein, 1985
p. 50

EMPIRICAL EVIDENCE indicates that patients with severe psychological illness are indeed able to understand and integrate interpretive comments, particularly if their understanding of the therapist's interpretations is examined and interpreted in turn. . . . The patient's difficulty in integrating verbal communication is itself a product of primitive defensive operations that can be interpreted, particularly as they are activated in the patient's reactions to the therapist's interpretations.

Otto Kernberg, 1982
p. 33

. . . INTERPRETATIONS have to be formulated so that the patient's distortions of the analyst's intervention can be simultaneously and systematically examined, and the patient's distortion of present reality and especially of his perceptions in the hour can be systematically clarified. This clarification does not mean suggestion, advice giving, or revelation regarding personal matters of the analyst to the patient, but a clear explanation of how the analyst sees the "here and now" interaction with the patient in contrast to how the analyst assumes the patient is interpreting this "here and now" interaction.

Otto Kernberg, 1975
p. 130

ALL BUT THE most disturbed patients need more to correct their distortions than they need a real object in the therapist.

Gertrude and Rubin Blanck, 1974
p. 187

... INTERPRETATIONS should help patients to recognize, accept, and modify their own activity in the creation and maintenance of their difficulties. Because people so often experience their problems as unwanted afflictions over which they have little or no control, an important principle of interpreting is the unmasking of their active, if often hidden participation in their problems.

Steven Levy, 1984
p. 65

THE FIRST PHASE of the interpretive process with regard to character problems is to make the patient aware of that aspect of their character that is interfering. The goal here is to make something that has been automatic and natural feeling to the patient stand out from the rest of his behavior. . . . Early character interpretations should merely call the patient's attention to what he is doing, with some indication, either explicit or implicit, that this is but one of several things he might choose to do. . . . A comment from the therapist, such as "so you are also tender and emotional," can help an overly controlled and severe patient recognize that he is making choices in being controlled and severe.

Steven Levy, 1984
p. 148

INTERPRETATIONS which connect the *actual life situation* with *past experiences* and with the *transference situation* — since the latter is always the axis around which such connections can best be made — I should like to call *total interpretations*. The more interpretations approximate this principle of totality, the more they fulfil their double purpose: they accelerate the assimilation of new material by the ego and mobilize further unconscious material.

Franz Alexander, 1935
p. 609

I DEFINE INSIGHT as the recognition by the patient (1) that this or that aspect of his feelings and attitudes, this or that technique of behavior, this or that role in which he casts other people, is *of a pattern*; (2) that this pattern, like the footprint of a bear which has lost certain toes in a trap, originated long ago and stamps itself on every step of his life journey; it is present in his contemporary reality situation relationships, and it is present in his analytic relationships; (3) that this pattern originated for a reason which was valid at the time, and persisted despite changes in some of the circumstances which originally determined it; (4) that this pattern contains elements which are offensive and injurious to others as well as expensive and troublesome to the patient.

Karl Menninger, 1958
pp. 147–148

MANY ANALYSTS, and I am one of them, believe that the only therapeutically meaningful interpretation is the interpretation of the transference.

Peter Giovacchini, 1979
p. 447

. . . THE PRIME ESSENTIAL of a transference interpretation in my view is that the feeling or impulse interpreted should not merely be concerned with the analyst but that it should be in activity at the moment at which it is interpreted. Thus an interpretation of an impulse felt towards the analyst last week or even a quarter of an hour ago will not be a transference interpretation in my sense unless it is . . . active in the patient at the moment when the interpretation is given. The situation will be, so to speak, a dead one and will be entirely without the dynamic force which is inherent in the giving of a true transference-interpretation.

James Strachey, 1937
p. 141

斗

... IT IS LESS easy for the patient, in the case of an extra-transference interpretation, to become directly aware of the distinction between the real object and the phantasy object. . . .In other words, an extra-transference interpretation is liable to be both less effective and more risky than a transference one.

James Strachey, 1934
pp. 154–155

斗

GIVING non-transference-interpretations is, in fact, like trying to untie a knot in an endless ring or rope. You can untie the knot quite easily in one place, but it will re-tie itself at the very same moment in some other part of the ring. You cannot really untie the knot unless you have hold of the ends of the rope, and that is your situation only when you make a transference-interpretation.

James Strachey, 1937
p. 143

斗

INTERPRETATION AND DEPRIVATION

... AN INTERPRETATION robs the patient of something. Patients do not welcome interpretations because you take something away from them, you take away some defensive structure or some disguised method of finding happiness. You are helpful but you are mean.

Sidney Tarachow, 1963
p. 267

斗

TO BEGIN WITH, every interpretation is a deprivation. This is more so in certain types of patients than others, especially for those who act out. Nevertheless every interpretation is designed to rob the patient of something—his fantasies, his defenses, his gratifications. Analysis and, to varying extents, psychotherapy involve real disappointment.

Sidney Tarachow, 1963
p. 13

⊐

... WE MUST NOT forget that the relationship between analyst and patient rests on the love of truth as its foundation, that is, on the acknowledgment of reality, and it precludes every sort of sham and deception.

Sigmund Freud, 1937
p. 401

⊐

RESIDENT: But some patients don't want to know the truth, do they?

Supervisor: That's so, but they signal that clearly. Don't worry. No matter what you do, those that don't want to know won't know, and I assure you they don't jump at the chance to explore what's happened to them. . . .

Michael Basch, 1980
p. 94

⊐

WHAT DOES NOT interest a patient cannot be forced upon him.

Otto Fenichel, 1941
p. 44

10

Countertransference

I ALWAYS RECALL the rejoinder of the late Dr. Elizabeth Zetzel to requests to smoke during the therapy hour. Dr Zetzel, a chainsmoker, puffed her way through sessions. In the midst of this cloud, when a patient asked if he or she could join in the activity, she refused permission. When the patient protested and noted her intense smoking, she explained: "What makes *you* anxious is good for the therapy. What makes *me* anxious is bad for the therapy!"

Sheldon Roth, 1987
p. 253

ⴄ

. . . THERAPY CANNOT proceed when the therapist is more anxious than the patient.

Jerome Kroll, 1988
p. 164

ⴄ

A PSYCHOANALYST is . . . nothing more than an artist at understanding, the product of an intensive course of study and training which has — if it has been successful — rendered him unusually sensitive to his fellow men. And it is this sensitivity — in short, the analyst's own person—which is the single instrument, the only tool, with which he performs. Only on himself, and on nothing else, does he depend.

Robert Lindner, 1982
pp. xxiv–xxv

⊐

W HEN THIS INTERNAL gyroscope seems to tilt to the left or right in response to some patient, this tilt becomes our first indication that a special process has been initiated in us. . . . At such times close acquaintance with ourselves is required. A sage cardiologist, early in my medical training, advised his young flock of aspirant physicians to study the normal heart, to listen again and again and never stop this activity, for then, the slightest abnormality would startle our senses, demanding that we seek its meaning and origin.

Sheldon Roth, 1987
p. 66

⊐

T HERE EXISTS IN most of us a tendency to avoid or deny counter-transference feelings. This is based on several factors. Primarily, it is due to the nature of the impulses themselves. What we repress in relation to our patients are the same incestuous, perverse, envious and vengeful desires that we prefer to not see in ourselves in any case. But also this denial is tolerated because it accords with certain highly unrealistic but socially accepted images of what a psychotherapist is or should be—calm, without anger or desire, mature, only a little neurotic. . . .

Winslow Hunt and Amnon Issacharoff, 1977
pp. 100–101

⊐

T HE PATIENT HAS to face a problem; and you have to face a problem. Every time you force a patient to understand something about himself, you are forcing yourself to a limited degree to tolerate a certain problem.

Sidney Tarachow, 1963
p. 26

⊐

... T HE THERAPIST inevitably has two patients to deal with, two people whose motivations he must scrutinize and understand—the patient and himself.

Erwin Singer, 1965
p. 163

⊐

... C OUNTER-TRANSFERENCE attitudes are deleterious to the process of therapy only to the extent to which they represent defensive and therefore unexamined attitudes and reactions.

Erwin Singer, 1965
p. 311

⊐

H OWEVER MUCH he loves his patients he cannot avoid hating them, and fearing them, and the better he knows this the less will hate and fear be the motive determining what he does to his patients.

D. W. Winnicott, 1949
p. 69

⊐

T HE PRINCIPAL temptation is to play the role of mother.

Sidney Tarachow, 1963
p. 14

W HEN THE PATIENT becomes an object mobilizing strong sexual feelings or aggression or guilt or anxiety, the patient has probably become a transference figure for the therapist.

Ralph Greenson, 1960
p. 420

⊒

A S WINNICOTT suggests, it is imperative that a parent or therapist be able to integrate his or her anger and murderous wishes toward their children and patients without enacting these feelings or having to get rid of them through denial and projection.

Thomas Ogden, 1979
p. 369

⊒

. . . H ATRED CAN ALSO be expressed by the therapist in a different way. He can worry about the patient. When instead of being angry at the patient you start worrying about him, it simply means that your hatred is even greater than when you are overtly angry. You are defending yourself even more against the hatred. Worry is the masochistic refuge of sadism. Worry is basically a sadistic attitude, just as pity is.

Sidney Tarachow, 1963
p. 250

⊒

HOSTILITY OF PATIENT TOWARD THERAPIST

T HERE IS NO way the analyst can avoid being hated. . . . To begin with, the analyst will be hated for daring to try to understand and formulate anything at all about the analysand, for any such activity threatens the status quo and is experienced as an attack.

Roy Schafer, 1983
p. 155

... T HE OVERLOOKING of the negative transference seems to be quite general. No doubt, this is due to our narcissism which makes us willing to listen to complimentary things but blind to negative attitudes unless they are expressed in more or less gross forms.

Wilhelm Reich, 1949
pp. 23–24

己

T HERE IS NO way around hostile activity on the analysand's part. There is only seduction away from this activity, as when the analyst treats the analysand as a fundamentally preconflictual being.

Roy Schafer, 1983
p. 78

己

T HE THERAPIST WHO makes warding-off comments the moment the patient expresses thoughts and feelings about the former as a person is not preventing transference complications; he is signaling that he is not competent and/or is too frightened to cope with the material that is coming to the surface. The result may be that the patient gets—and complies with—the message that he must back away from such material; the treatment then remains on a superficial level. . . . Inability and/or unwillingness to deal with the transference is probably the most common reason for the failure of psychotherapy—the cause of its becoming a boring, circular, repetitive recounting of symptoms, with emphasis on placing the blame for them on external situations, past and present.

Michael Basch, 1980
p. 40

THE FACT THAT the analyst feels uncomfortable is not the problem. It becomes a problem only when the analyst demands, or even simply expects, the patient to change in a fashion so that he will no longer feel uncomfortable.

Peter Giovacchini, 1979
p. 498

⊒

. . . JUST AS POSITIVE transference must be understood as a reflection of essentially negative attitudes, so positive counter-transference reveals the therapist's essentially defensive and negative orientation toward his patient.

Erwin Singer, 1965
p. 295

⊒

PATIENTS WHO typically flatter the therapist not only let him know about their own needs, but should also give the therapist some insight about himself, i.e., his apparent susceptibility to flattery.

Ernst Beier, 1966
p. 39

⊒

THE EVOLUTION OF THE CONCEPT OF
COUNTERTRANSFERENCE

As FAR As transference is concerned, it will be remembered that Freud saw it first as a hindrance, but later regarded it as an indispensable vehicle for the analytic work. However, he did not take a similar step in regard to countertransference . . . this inevitable step was taken after Freud.

Joseph Sandler, 1976
p. 43

IT HAS BEEN extremely difficult to make the shift from regarding the analyst's emotional or affective reactions as errors from which the patient naturally needs to be protected, to regarding these responses as significant data with a potential for illuminating the therapeutic situation. And Freud's ambivalence on this point certainly did not help.

Lawrence Epstein and Arthur Feiner, 1979
p. 506

ᘔ

. . . RACKER'S ELABORATION of countertransference theory, and of the use to which countertransference data may be put in clinical practice, remains probably the most comprehensive and original contribution by any single author.

Lawrence Epstein and Arthur Feiner, 1979
p. 490

ᘔ

RACKER'S . . . EMPHASIS was on the patient's role, at every moment, in creating the therapist's affective state. His central thesis is that there is no "normal" emotional state for the therapist, but that the therapist's inner state is continuously, profoundly, and in certain precise and definable ways, responsive to the patient and to what the patient is saying and doing. The patient influences the emotions of the therapist to a degree and in ways not previously appreciated. Even when the therapist seems detached and calmly analytic, closer study of the total situation will usually reveal that the detachment is in itself a defensive maneuver responsive to something the patient is doing. It might be, for instance, a retaliatory withdrawal from a patient who is emotionally flat, i.e., who deprives the therapist of affective stimuli and a human relationship.

Winslow Hunt and Amnon Issacharoff, 1977
p. 95

THE CONCEPT OF countertransference led the way out of a narrow one-body, intrapsychic psychology to an extraordinarily complex two-body psychology, which explores the effects of two psyches in mutual interaction.

Sheldon Roth, 1987
p. 45

WHEN THE ANALYST feels that his emotional reaction is an important technical instrument for understanding and helping the patient, the analyst feels freer to face his positive and negative emotions evoked in the transference situation, has less need to block these reactions, and can utilize them for his analytic work.

Otto Kernberg, 1965
p. 40

THE KINDS OF questions I always direct to another therapist concern "what was it like for you to be with this patient?"

Lane Gerber, 1974/1975
p. 60

ONCE THE ANALYST has identified his own emotional state, he is able to consider the questions, why have I fallen into this position now? What has this to do with the analytic process? What internal self and object relations might the patient be enacting with me? Do my feelings indicate that he needs my love, or that he wants to triumph over me? Is the patient from the position of his child-self relating to me as if I were his superego? Do my feelings indicate that he wants me to punish, or criticize, or demean him?

Lawrence Epstein and Arthur Feiner, 1979
p. 496

THOUGH THE mechanism of emphatic regression in the analyst, certain conflicts of the patient may reactivate similar conflicts of the analyst's past; this regression may also reactivate previously abandoned, old character defenses of the analyst. . . . When strong negative countertransference reactions extend over a long period of time, whatever their origin, the analyst may revert to former neurotic patterns in his interaction with a particular patient which had been given up in his contact with other patients and in his life outside the analytic hours. The analyst, so to speak, becomes his worst in his relationship with a certain patient.

Otto Kernberg, 1965
p. 42

⊐

WE CAN HARDLY be surprised if constant pre-occupation with all the repressed impulses which struggle for freedom in the human psyche sometimes causes all the instinctual demands which have hitherto been restrained to be violently awakened in the analyst himself.

Sigmund Freud, 1937
p. 402

⊐

AS WE PROCEED from the "neurotic pole" of the continuum toward the "psychotic pole," transference manifestations become increasingly predominant in the patient's contribution to the countertransference reaction of the therapist, displacing the importance of those counter-transference aspects which arise from the therapist's past.

Otto Kernberg, 1965
p. 43

W HEN DEALING with borderline or severely regressed patients, as contrasted to those presenting symptomatic neuroses and many character disorders, the therapist tends to experience rather soon in the treatment intensive emotional reactions having more to do with the patient's premature, intense and chaotic transference, and with the therapist's capacity to withstand psychological stress and anxiety, than with any particular, specific problem of the therapist's past. . . . Given reasonably well-adjusted therapists, all hypothetically dealing with the same severely regressed and disorganized patient, their counter-transference reactions will be somewhat similar, reflecting the patient's problems much more than any specific problem of the analyst's past.

Otto Kernberg, 1965
p. 43

W E HAVE . . . been made aware of the fact that our more intense countertransference reactions are usually generated by the more severely disturbed type of patient. Thus, countertransference is now seen as a normal, natural interpersonal event, rather than an idiosyncratic pathological phenomenon.

Lawrence Epstein and Arthur Feiner, 1979
p. 508

COUNTERTRANSFERENCE AND IDENTIFICATION

"C ONCORDANT identification," according to Racker, is an identification of the analyst with the corresponding part of the patient's psychic apparatus: ego with ego, superego with superego. Under the influence of concordant identification, the analyst experiences in himself the central emotion that the patient is experiencing at the same time. . . . "Complementary identification" (a concept first expressed by Helene Deutsch) refers to the identification of the analyst with the transference objects of the patient. In that position, the analyst experiences the emotion that the patient is putting into his transference object, while the patient himself is experiencing the emotion which he had experienced in the past in his interaction with that particular parental image. . . . Racker states that the analyst fluctuates between these two kinds of counter-transference identifications.

Otto Kernberg, 1965
p. 49

⊐

ALTHOUGH THE purposes of conceptual clarity are perhaps best served by distinguishing between patient-induced and therapist-related countertransference, it is often difficult to determine in any given practical situation just how much of the therapist's reaction to the patient's behavior is an understandable response (patient-induced countertransference) and how much is a function of the therapist's own unique personality (therapist-related countertransference). . . . It could perhaps be argued that the therapist's reactions to his patients are always a combination of patient-induced and therapist-related countertransference, although in some situations the contribution of one of the two components might be very small.

Daniel Wile, 1972
p. 39

⊐

WHEN I ONCE said to Fairbairn, "Countertransference must be harmful to a patient," he replied, "You may do more harm to a patient if you are too afraid of countertransference."

Harry Guntrip, 1969
p. 334

Y OU CAN EXERT no influence if you are not susceptible to influence.

Carl Jung, 1933
p. 49

11

Treatment
of Severe
Disturbance

ONCE A PRINCE went crazy and convinced himself that he was a turkey. He took off all his clothes and sat naked under the table, and refused to eat any real food. He put into his mouth only some oats and tiny bits of bone.

His father, the king, brought all the doctors to cure him, but they could do nothing. Finally, one wise man came to the King and said, "I take it upon myself to cure your son."

Right away the wise man took off all his clothes, sat under the table next to the prince and began collecting oats and bits of bone, and putting them into his mouth.

The prince asked him, "Who are you? What are you doing here?" The wise man responded, "Who are you? What are you doing here?" The prince answered, "I am a turkey." The wise man said, "I also am a turkey."

The two turkeys sat together until they got used to each other. Once the wise man saw this, he hinted to the King to bring him a shirt. The wise man put it on, and he said to the prince, "Do you think that a turkey isn't allowed to wear a shirt? He is allowed, and if he wears one, he is not any less a turkey." These words the prince took to heart and he agreed to wear a shirt, too.

A few days later, the wise man hinted to the King to bring him a pair of pants. He put them on, and said to the prince, "Do you think that a turkey is forbidden to wear pants? Even if he wears pants, he is still a full-fledged turkey." The prince admitted that this was true, and he too started wearing pants.

This went on, step by step, until finally, having followed the wise man's instructions, the prince was wearing a full set of clothes. Later, the wise man asked that human food be served on top of the table. He took some and ate it, and he said to the prince, "Do you think that a turkey is forbidden to eat some good food? One can eat the best food in the world and still be a true-blooded turkey." The prince accepted this, too, and began eating like a human being.

Once the wise man saw this, he said to the prince, "Do you really think that a turkey must sit under the table? No, not necessarily so! A turkey can walk around wherever he likes and no one holds it against him." The prince pondered this and accepted the wise man's view. And once he stood up and walked like a human being, he began acting like a real human being and forgot that he was a turkey.

The prince in the tale has regressed to some earlier infantile, naked state of life. He rules a childish realm beneath the protective roof of a maternal symbol, the table, upon which the parental nourishment of food is set. In this state he is stubborn and negativistic and exhibits his distress before all. What has caused the regression is unclear from the tale. Exactly why the regression moved to this level is also unclear. What is clear is that the prince has left himself in a dependent position relative to those around him, while apparently rejecting help. This is a classic position for many psychotic patients.

From our modern point of view, the actions of the wise man are uncanny. It is as if he had read Freud and Searles . . . possibly even the Existentialists, since knowing and judging are put aside in the interests of being and sharing. He works slowly with little confrontation, takes the empathic position, and allows the prince to move from a neutral observing position to a slow symbiosis and fusion, whereby he and the prince both experience themselves as turkeys. Only when this turkey-transference symbiosis has been achieved does the sage behave in ways that are basically action–interpretations aimed at separation and individuation.

Sheldon Roth, 1987
pp. 41–43

I N THE SCHIZOPHRENIAS and the delinquences the whole technique must be changed in all essential aspects.

Kurt Eissler, 1953
pp. 113–114

🝫

. . . C LINICAL experience shows that there is a group of patients whose treatment does need scarcely more than interpretation to usher in the process of recovery and to lead the ego to the therapeutic goal. . . . This group has an important structural factor in common — a relatively unmodified ego.

Kurt Eissler, 1953
p. 126

🝫

T HE BASIC MODEL technique, without emendations, can be applied to those patients whose neurotic symptomatology is borne by an ego not modified to any noteworthy degree. . . . If the ego has preserved its integrity, it will make maximum use of the support it receives from the analyst in the form of interpretation.

Kurt Eissler, 1953
p. 116

🝫

PRIMITIVE CHARACTER STRUCTURES

. . . T HEY CANNOT reconcile conflicting trends within themselves, not because of the nature of the conflicts, but rather because they do not have the equipment to do so.

Steven Levy, 1984
p. 156

It used to be said that an "intact ego" is a precondition for psycho-analysis. But in the light of the most recent psychoanalytical advances, it is precisely this that is so hard to find. We are much more likely today than were the earlier analytical therapists to find ourselves coming upon indubitable signs of basic ego-weakness obtruding into the middle of oedipal analysis.

Harry Guntrip, 1969
p. 317

⊒

In other words it would be pleasant if we were to be able to take for analysis only those patients whose mothers at the very start and also in the first months had been able to provide good enough conditions. But this era of psycho-analysis is steadily drawing to a close.

D. W. Winnicott, 1955
p. 24

⊒

There is a vast difference between those patients who have had satisfactory early experiences which can be discovered in the transference, and those whose very early experiences have been so deficient or distorted that the analyst has to be the first in the patient's life to supply certain environmental essentials.

D. W. Winnicott, 1949
p. 72

⊒

We know that there are fairly great difficulties when "the child in our patient" is of the age of the Oedipus conflict. But the gulf separating us adults from "the child in our patient" of the age of the basic fault—the "infant" in the true sense of the word . . . is considerably deeper. . . . The gulf separating patient and analyst must be bridged if the therapeutic work is to continue. It must be realized, however, that the patient—that is, "the child in the patient" of the age of the basic fault—is unable to bridge the gulf on his own. The great technical question is, how to bridge this gulf? Which part of this task should be undertaken by the analyst and which should be left to the patient?

Michael Balint, 1968
p. 90

己

THE FIRST ANSWER to the problem, how to bridge the gap, is the standard one: by understanding what the patient needs from the analyst. This understanding need not—and at times definitely must not—be conveyed to a regressed patient by interpretations but by creating the atmosphere that he needs.

Michael Balint, 1968
p. 82

己

FAILURES IN ANALYSIS

OUR TECHNIQUE was worked out for patients who experience the analyst's interpretation as interpretation and whose ego is strong enough to enable them to "take in" the interpretation and perform what Freud called the process "working-through." We know that not every patient is capable of this task, and it is with these patients that we encounter difficulties.

Michael Balint, 1968
p. 10

己

IN OTHER WORDS, in order to use a transference interpretation, the patient must have a capacity for illusion, play, and self-reflection—all of which was missing in this patient.

Andrew Druck, 1989
p. 181

W ORKING-THROUGH can come into operation only if our words have approximately the same meaning for our patients as for ourselves. No such problem exists at the oedipal level. The patient and his analyst confidently speak the same language; the same words mean about the same for both. True, the patient may reject an interpretation, may be annoyed, frightened, or hurt by it, but there is no question that it *was* an interpretation.

Michael Balint, 1968
p. 14

O N MANY OCCASIONS I have found to my annoyance and despair that words cease to be reliable means of communication when the analytic work reaches the areas beyond the oedipal level. The analyst may try, as hard as he can, to make his interpretations clear and unequivocal; the patient, somehow, always manages to experience them as something utterly different from that which the analyst intended them to be. At this level . . . words become, in fact, unreliable and unpredictable.

Michael Balint, 1968
p. 174

[T HE PATIENT] will need many years of ego-building psychotherapy before interpretation of oedipal wishes will be useful. In fact, in many such cases this point is never reached and therapy ends successfully with a stronger ego, higher level of object relations, lessened anxiety, firmer sense of identity, but not necessarily with the uncovering of

unconscious fantasies. And so the royal road is sometimes not trav-
eled, but other highways are chosen because they lead to destinations
more desirable than direct access to the id.

Gertrude and Rubin Blanck, 1974
pp. 239–240

▤

... PSYCHOANALYTICAL theory today centers less and less on the
control of instinct and more on the development of a stable core of
selfhood—that is, the laying of the foundations of a strong personal
ego in a good mother–infant relationship at the start of life, and its
subsequent fate in the ever varying types of personal relationships,
good and bad, that make up our life.

Harry Guntrip, 1971
pp. 12–13

▤

THE ANALYST'S role in certain periods of new beginning resembles in
many respects that of the primary substances or objects. He must be
there; he must be pliable to a very high degree; he must not offer much
resistance; he certainly must be indestructible, and he must allow his
patient to live with him in a sort of harmonious interpenetrating
mix-up. I know this sounds rather comical and I am prepared for a
goodly number of well-aimed jokes commenting on this new technique, but may I plead that I am trying to render into words experiences that belong to a period well before—or beyond—the discovery of
words, and largely even before the emergence of objects. . . .

Michael Balint, 1968
p. 136

▤

THE AREA OF BASIC FAULT

IT IS DEFINITELY a two-person relationship in which, however, only one
of the partners matters; his wishes and needs are the only ones that

count and must be attended to; the other partner, though felt to be immensely powerful, matters only in so far as he is willing to gratify the first partner's needs and desires or decides to frustrate them; beyond this his personal interests, needs, desires, wishes, etc., simply do not exist.

Michael Balint, 1968
p. 23

⊒

NONE OF THE details of the therapeutic attitude . . . are essentially different from what the analyst adopts when dealing with patients at the oedipal level, and even the topics worked with are usually the same; but there is a difference, which is more a difference of atmosphere, of mood. . . . The analyst is not so keen on "understanding" everything immediately, and in particular, on "organizing" and changing everything undesirable by his correct interpretations; in fact, he is more tolerant towards the patient's sufferings and is capable of bearing with them—i.e., of admitting his relative impotence— instead of being at pains to "analyse" them away in order to prove his therapeutic omnipotence.

Michael Balint, 1968
p. 184

⊒

A BELIEF IN human nature and in the developmental process exists in the analyst if work is to be done at all, and this is quickly sensed by the patient.

D. W. Winnicott, 1955
p. 25

⊒

SOME MAINTAIN that an attitude of neutrality . . . [is appropriate] . . . only for analysis of neurotic patients, and that therapy of more severely ill patients must add supportive measures in which the analyst takes over ego functions and parental functions for the patient. I strongly disagree; respect for the patient's autonomy is an even more critical issue in the treatment of severely ill patients.

Theodore Dorpat, 1977
p. 54

PSYCHOANALYTIC teaching has always emphasized the importance of the analyst as the guardian of autonomy. I would add that it is critical that the therapist also bear the responsibility of being the guardian of the self. . . . I believe that the single, most critical and powerful message that one can communicate to the borderline patient—or indeed to any patient with a character disorder—is one's concern for and dedication to the survival of the self. The therapeutic alliance depends ultimately upon this fundamental trust.

Althea Horner, 1980
p. 195

TO BREAK DOWN inhibition, to encourage closeness, to attack defenses, to ventilate unneutralized libido and aggression, are not ego building. In fact, for the nonneurotic patient, it is a necessary therapeutic goal to help to acquire distance from the other person as part of the process of acquiring identity. The aloof patient is usually so because he has no objects or, if less disturbed than that, because, by maintaining distance, he is defending against loss of identity through merger. In either type of structure, psychotic or borderline, forcing closeness is harmful; ventilation exposes the ego to more than it can tolerate, exhilarating as such experience may be. . . . The mechanical principle that a person, like a steam engine, needs to blow off, refutes itself as soon as it is stated.

Gertrude and Rubin Blanck, 1974
p. 216

VERBAL ABUSE OF THE THERAPIST

N OT ONLY IS IT therapeutically valueless in and of itself, but it places the therapist in a denigrated, masochistic-like role which will preclude positive identifications later on.

Gertrude and Rubin Blanck, 1974
p. 352

⊐

. . . T REATMENT OF the very severely disturbed patient involves the use of the therapist as a real object for the purpose of building object relations.

Gertrude and Rubin Blanck, 1974
p.76

⊐

I T IS NOT useful to challenge the patient's convictions about important relationships too early. . . . Object relations, even cathexis of a negative object, must be maintained.

Gertrude and Rubin Blanck, 1974
p. 102

⊐

. . . N EGATIVE AND distorted self and object representations can be dealt with therapeutically only after a solid foundation of positive self and object representations is provided. One never assures the patient that the parents were better and more loving than they really were, but one does seek out those areas, no matter how minimal, in which they did function as good parents, thus providing the patient with a base that will make tolerable knowing also where they failed.

Gertrude and Rubin Blanck, 1974
p. 124

THE RELIABILITY OF THE THERAPIST

... THE UNWAVERING reliability of the therapist is essential to building object relations. The therapist is there, predictable, in the same kindly mood each time. Pressure of need gratification diminishes in such a climate. The energy used in forcing minimal gratification from the object becomes neutralized.

Gertrude and Rubin Blanck, 1974
p. 339

... REGULARITY OF appointments with the analyst always becomes equivalent to the analyst's continuous presence. . . .

Heinz Kohut, 1971
p. 120

... THE MANNER IN which the analyst or therapist establishes and maintains the ground rules and boundaries of the therapeutic setting and interaction is among the most important means through which he conveys to the patient the essence of his identity and the dynamic state of his own intrapsychic structures, conflicts, and balances.

Robert Langs, 1975
p. 107

IT IS EVIDENT to me that every patient has an identifiable, predictable, and intense response to the slightest deviation in the framework of the therapeutic relationship.

Robert Langs, 1975
p. 115

LIMITS

TESTING THE LIMITS, yes. That's one thing that patients do from the beginning.

Robert Langs, 1976
p. 20

ㄹ

THE PATIENT, child or adult, will derive from limits imposed the relieving sense that he is not omnipotent. Contrary to the often-voiced and popular belief—prevalent even among the psychologically sophisticated—the feeling of omnipotence is most disturbing and troublesome human experiences imaginable, because it entails feelings of unreality and paradoxically a sense of nothingness and nonexistence.

Michael Basch, 1980
p. 156

ㄹ

SOME PATIENTS attempt to infringe unreasonably upon the time of other patients by trying to stay for longer than the appointed time. . . . The setting of limits in these instances is important. . . . Such limits will convince the patient more than words that the therapist genuinely respects the rights of others, and this genuinely protective attitude furthers the patient's development of trust in the therapist's rational concern with him personally.

Erwin Singer, 1965
p. 156

ㄹ

DEVELOPMENT is best promoted within a consistent, positive, reliable therapeutic climate which contains tolerable doses of frustration. It is the experience of frustration that promotes differentiation of self and object representations.

Gertrude and Rubin Blanck, 1974
p. 173

Occasionally a patient asks fairly urgently at the last moment if he can see the doctor on the next day, looking as if he were having violent anxiety, and were preparing to do something about it. My suggestion in such a case is to indicate a time on the next day when the patient can call to find out if you have time for a session. There will probably be a lucid interval, perhaps when he is on his way home, or when he is going to bed that night, during which he can take stock of what has happened. If, after this stock-taking, he still wants to see you next day, he can always call up and find out if it is possible. But if he actually feels greatly reassured as a result of the lucid interval, and you have already agreed to his request, he may feel somewhat like a fool; and, incidentally, since it is unpleasant to feel like a fool, he may wonder whether you, the expert, may not be a bit of a fool too, or whether you have nothing to do except run in emergency appointments next day.

Harry Stack Sullivan, 1954
p. 217

THE NEUROTIC patient need not know where the therapist goes on vacation. His intact ego encompasses continuous existence of stable object representations. The decision about whether and how much to tell other patients has to be made . . . upon appraisal of the level of development and of the ego's capacity to sustain constant object representations.

Gertrude and Rubin Blanck, 1974
p. 182

FREE ASSOCIATION is useful when there is uncovering to be done by an ego that is capable of adequate defense and that operates in the secondary process most of the time.

Gertrude and Rubin Blanck, 1974
p. 128

V ERBALIZATION is a complex of ego functions including such major ones as symbolization, delay, interposition of thought before action and of object relations. As the ego is encouraged to exercise, its functioning improves and structuralization proceeds.

Gertrude and Rubin Blanck, 1974
p. 162

⊒

. . . T HE REAL TECHNICAL purpose of verbalization is to bring heretofore unmentioned, often preverbal, material under the aegis of the ego. It is the ego that has to communicate semantically with the therapist, calling into play all the auxiliary ego functions we have mentioned as contributory to the complex process of verbalization — symbolization, intentionality, object relations, and so forth. Particularly does verbalization aid neutralization because the drive energy that might otherwise be discharged motorically or through physiological channels becomes available for transfer to the ego. In addition, ideation becomes bound in the secondary process when it is put into words. Verbalization also promotes capacity to delay by building frustration tolerance. The short circuit of impulse discharge is rewired to go through a central controlling mechanism — the ego.

Gertrude and Rubin Blanck, 1974
pp. 348–349

⊒

V ERBALIZATION protects identity by guarding privacy. The fact that one has to convey one's thoughts to another person implies differentiation of self and other.

Gertrude and Rubin Blanck, 1974
p. 216

T IMING IS OFTEN a matter of waiting, even if we think we have a clever thought, until the patient is near it himself. A patient is asked what his material might mean. He says, typically, "I don't know." The therapist says, "Try." Simple, but effective in ego building. . . . To urge the patient along, it seems to us, is more than encouragement. It gently refuses to do the therapeutic work for him so that he gains confidence in his own ability instead of remaining fixated in admiration of a brilliant therapist who makes interpretations that he, the patient, could never match.

Gertrude and Rubin Blanck, 1974
p. 326

D ON'T SAY "CAN you" because that implies maybe she can't. Always assume she can — everyone can, is, will be — that's the basic assumption from which you operate.

James Masterson, 1983
p. 32

T HE SIMPLE PHRASE "at least" cannot be overused in supporting the ego at its optimal level of functioning. In that way, patient and therapist get together in appreciation of the development which has been reached, making possible its becoming the foundation stone for further development. This is the true meaning of "ego support." It addresses itself to the highest level of development the way a builder shores up the last story of a building in order to proceed to building the next story. It differs from random support in its precision and specificity, and from praise, which is therapeutically worthless and is usually perceived by the patient as false.

Gertrude and Rubin Blanck, 1974
p. 250

T HE WORK OF treatment itself must convey . . . the very quiet, consistent assumption that problems can be handled, tolerated, dealt with, and worked through. Your patient identifies not only with your verbal interventions but also with your manner and attitude.

James Masterson, 1983
p. 53

F OCUSSING ON how the patient utilizes the psychotherapeutic work in between the hours is of utmost importance in assessing the development of an observing ego and of the therapeutic alliance, and also, of the more subtle types of negative therapeutic reaction (unconscious tendencies to destroy or neutralize the emotional meaning and the learning that has gone on in the hours).

Otto Kernberg, 1975
p. 187

. . . T HESE KINDS OF patients experienced terrible deprivations and traumas at the hands of their parents. . . . In order for them to get better, they have to be able to face their feelings about that and work them through. To do that they need you there, not saying, "There, there now, etc.," but rather, using your empathy to discipline yourself so that you don't do that. Instead, you sit there and require, by your interventions, that they work it through. In this way you really offer them something. And there is no other way. Nowhere is it written that life is just; injustice happens, and you have to deal with it. Eventually, your patient learns that.

James Masterson, 1983
p. 25

You KNOW THAT I always say, "Don't verbally reassure patients." However, enormous reassurance and strength are conveyed by this quiet assumption: "We are here to work on your problems." The patient identifies with this, and the anxiety tones down.

James Masterson, 1983
p. 12

⊇

IN ORDER TO achieve improvement in distorted ego functions, the patient must come to terms at some point with very real, serious limitations of what life has given him in his early years.

Otto Kernberg, 1975
p. 174

⊇

COMING TO TERMS with severe defects in one's past requires the capacity to mourn and to work through such mourning; to accept aloneness; and to realistically accept that others may have what the patient himself may never be able to fully compensate for.

Otto Kernberg, 1975
p. 175

⊇

BECAUSE OF THE trauma these patients have experienced as children, one of their principal motivations in life, when they become parents, is to not repeat with their children what happened to them as children; inevitably they do. However, this becomes a powerful motivation in treatment. . . . When you confront her with the fact that she's not doing what she thinks she ought to for her kids, it reinforces this basic motivation. With some patients in intensive analytic treatment, the strongest and most effective confrontations often are those having to do with their children.

James Masterson, 1983
p. 28

〓

O NE OF THE major perils of our pharmacological culture is the avoidance of development—preventing frustration with the help of tranquilizers or amphetamines. The result is disturbed structure formation and disorder in ego and superego development.

Gertrude and Rubin Blanck, 1974
p. 50

〓

Y OU ARE ACTIVE and confronting when the patient is unable to do it for herself. You are supplying something that is required, as the work won't be done without it. When that confrontation is integrated and the patient starts to do it for herself, you no longer do it for her; you back out.

James Masterson, 1983
p. 24

〓

B Y CORRECTLY labeling seemingly unrelated behaviors as examples of a few central themes, therapist and patient are able to gain perspective on what are otherwise a kaleidoscope of overwhelming events and emotions.

Jerome Kroll, 1988
p. 166

〓

MANAGEMENT OF PROJECTION

... A SAFE COURSE for the analyst to follow when he is the depository of the patient's projections is, first, to contain the projections, and then, to restrict his comments and questions to those which are directed away from the patient's ego and toward his own ego. If the patient, for instance, finds fault with the analyst or impugns his motives or intentions, the patient's perceptions and ideas should not be challenged; they should either be reflected—e.g., "you mean, I am such-and-such a kind of person," or "I'm really out to get you"—or they should be objectively investigated: he can be asked, for example to describe the analyst's faults more fully and asked for his ideas on how they should be corrected. He can be asked to elaborate on his ideas concerning the analyst's motives and whether he thinks they are conscious or unconscious, and asked in a non-challenging way if he can describe any of the evidence upon which he is basing his conclusions. . . . The question of how much of that which the patient attributes to the analyst is distorted or reality-based is treated as irrelevant. All of the patient's ideas and perceptions are taken seriously. This approach reduces paranoid anxiety because it steadily conveys the reassurance that the analyst has been unharmed by the patient's projections and is more interested in understanding him and in investigating his projections than in counter-attacking and punishing.

Lawrence Epstein, 1979
p. 265

. . . WE MAY FEEL vitiated, controlled, and threatened and our own survival needs may impel us to rid ourselves of the patient's projections so that we can experience the relief of feeling ourselves again. And this is true whether the patient makes of us a devil or an angel. The act of interpreting at such moments, then, may be an *unwitting acting-out* of our need both to rid ourselves of the unwanted projections and to attack the patient for what he is doing to us.

Lawrence Epstein, 1979
p. 262

T HE THERAPIST'S technique continuously drew out the patient's projections of her own insufficiencies until her ego was ready to take them
back. In the process, the therapist said nothing to challenge the
accuracy of the patient's perception of her . . . nor did she say anything that might invalidate such negative feelings and judgements. To
have done so might have induced the premature return of the patient's
badness to her ego.

Lawrence Epstein, 1979
p. 255

〓

. . . [T HUS] THE ANALYST must sincerely accept all complaints, re-
criminations, and resentments as real and valid, and allow ample time
to his patient to change his violent resentment into regret. This
process must not be hurried by interpretations, however correct, since
they may be felt as undue interference, as an attempt at devaluing the
justification of their complaint and thus, instead of speeding up, they
will slow down the therapeutic processes.

Michael Balint, 1968
p. 182

〓

MANAGEMENT OF ACTING-OUT

I F A PATIENT has a history of frequent suicidal attempts, or of utilizing
threats of suicide to control his environment (including the psychotherapist), this situation needs to be discussed fully with him. The
patient must either be able to assume full control over any active
expression of his suicidal tendencies (in contrast to the freedom of
verbally expressing his wishes and impulses in the treatment hours), or
he must be willing to ask for external protection (in the form of
hospitalization or part-hospitalization) if he feels he cannot control
such suicidal impulses.

Otto Kernberg, 1975
pp. 190–191

... SETTING LIMITS ahead of time for situations which may develop in the future constitutes a parameter of technique which needs to be formulated early, before the more intense transference distortions develop which may complicate such a prohibition in the future. . . . Patients with a history of cutting themselves may require a careful discussion at the beginning of treatment of the probability that the urges to cut themselves may recur and become very intense at some stage in the treatment. The therapist may have to express firmly his expectation that the patient will candidly discuss such wishes to cut himself in the hours and assume the responsibility for not acting on them; or, if he feels he cannot control such impulses, request hospitalization at that time. Throughout such discussions, the psychotherapist makes it clear that he expects the patient to express himself verbally rather than in action.

Otto Kernberg, 1975
pp. 192–193

IN GENERAL, IT is our task during the entire therapy to demand a limitation on any behavior on the part of the patient that is future– foreclosing either of the patient's career or life or therapy. This limitation comes first and nothing else should be discussed in the therapy until it is observed; if the patient refuses to limit such activities no therapy can take place. Actually the ultimate test of whether the patient is really motivated for psychotherapy comes in his willingness to limit self-destructive behavior.

Richard Chessick, 1979
p. 535

IN ALL GRADES of severity of acting-out, it is important to establish continuity for the patient in place of the discontinuity that exists through his use of denial, magical thinking, and other distortion.

Leopold Bellak and Peri Faithorn, 1981
p. 55

ACTING-OUT . . . implies poor *ego functions*, above all, poor *impulse* control and *poor judgment*. Typically, people who are acting out may be vaguely aware that they may not be doing the best or wisest thing; however, at the same time, there is the feeling that, in this special situation, the behavior makes sense, is justifiable or a good thing to do. Under such circumstances there is a definite defect in judgment under the impact of very urgent impulses. The hallmarks of acting-out are *urgency* and *impulsivity*.

Leopold Bellak and Peri Faithorn, 1981
p. 105

ONE OF THE most effective ways to deal with acting-out is to systematically and intentionally predict for the patient under what circumstances he is likely to act out. By getting the specific details of events surrounding the acting-out, the analyst can usually find clues as to what precipitates the process of acting-out and can clearly predict that the patient will behave the same way again when he encounters the same situation. The analyst, of course, couches this in hopes that his prediction will turn out to be wrong. This increases signal awareness of cues that are likely to forewarn acting-out, and such awareness, combined with making the behavior ego-alien, will obviate the need for acting-out.

Leopold Bellak and Peri Faithorn, 1981
pp. 109–110

THE ANALYST can point out to the patient that he is almost forced, by his past history, to repeat his actions. Being thus programmed deprives him of freedom of choice. This intervention will often take away much of the fun involved in acting-out. A good deal of the pleasure of acting-out is the gratification of the impulse to do what one wants when one wants. Removal of the *narcissistic pleasure*, as well as the *magical implications*, is achieved by explanations and clarifications of the programmed nature of the activity.

Leopold Bellak and Peri Faithorn, 1981
p. 108

⊇

A T TIMES, THE therapist's functioning . . . will be severely tested. Can he meet patient's threats of abandoning the treatment, of entering into catastrophic relationships, of committing suicide, with interpretive interventions that make such crises understandable? When are other measures really necessary? No easy answers are available. Such patients often have poor prognoses, even in the best of hands. Many die by suicide or in accidents of one kind or another in which suicidal intent cannot be accurately assessed. The therapist may be unwilling or unable to tolerate the possibly disastrous outcomes of working with such patients. . . . Treatment of the kind described herein can only succeed if the therapist believes that the responsibility for the patient's safety and welfare lies primarily with the patient. If he does not feel this is the case, then he cannot respond interpretively to the events of treatment. And if he responds in some other way, the treatment usually deteriorates, the patient is in fact more endangered, and the therapeutic results will be negative.

Steven Levy, 1984
p. 159

⊇

T HE ACTUAL composition of a caseload has certain built-in limiting effects. Treating two, or at most three, actively suicidal out-patients will overwhelm most therapists. The strain of such cases is complex and intense, often requiring much telephone time. When we are in such a situation, we should not put ourselves in an untenable situation when offered another suicidal patient. It is not possible to handle more. The same holds true for impulsive, acting-out borderline personalities. Each such patient requires a long period of working-through until a stable relationship is established.

Sheldon Roth, 1987
p. 251

己

USE OF THE HOSPITAL

IF PSYCHOTHERAPY is indicated, and if the psychotherapy is unrealistically limited by premature acting out, hospitalization, even though stressful for the patient, is preferable to undertaking a psychotherapy within which the necessary structuring is interfered with by the same pathology for which definite structuring is indicated.

Otto Kernberg, 1975
p. 99

己

WHEN YOU USE a hospital for any more than riding over a crisis and attaching to a therapist, then you're not running a hospital, you're running a hotel.

Elvin Semrad, 1980
p. 182

己

COUNTERTRANSFERENCE in the hospital milieu is a whole topic unto itself. Disturbed patients who are hospitalized often have difficulty in integrating disparate and contradictory portions of their personality. They have trouble hating the person they love, so they look for someone to hate and another someone to love. . . . Stubborn, bitter struggles between therapist and various staff members may result, for the various ego states of the patient have been dealt out to a large number of staff members like a deck of cards, each recipient thinking him or herself the one with the winning hand.

Sheldon Roth, 1987
p. 63

In MY EARLY years of practice, I conducted treatment exclusively in the one-to-one relationship. I now use the group therapeutic setting as well. . . . I have found the dyad to be the preferred setting for patients with the preoedipal disorders. But the results achieved to date in exposing some of these patients to both settings, concurrently or in sequence, suggest that a highly specific combination of individual and group therapy will eventually emerge as the treatment of choice for the most severe disorders.

Hyman Spotnitz, 1976
p. 17

TREATMENT OF DECOMPENSATED PATIENTS

Without discouraging exploration and interpretation of fascinating psychotic presentations of psychodynamics, and without reducing its importance for the long-range goals of treatment, we must realize that the most important activity taking place early in treatment is that a dedicated therapist is listening. Attachment is fighting the regressive trend toward isolation and withdrawal. The patient's and the therapist's speech is a vehicle for attachment.

Sheldon Roth, 1987
p. 167

A PERSON WILL resort to psychotic defenses when more usual ways of coping fail. Consequently, when the ardent practitioner of mental health is eager to quell the ravages of psychosis, its functional aspect must be kept in mind. Psychosis is an obscuring night of safety. If this protective cloak is taken from the patient too rapidly, the patient may become anxious over what will replace it.

Sheldon Roth, 1987
p. 236

目

IN BETWEEN psychosis and compensation, patients are like persons undergoing surgery. They feel their life and consciousness are in the hands of the surgeon; they require great and gentle reassurance that they will neither be abandoned nor left vulnerable in this strange state of altered consciousness.

Sheldon Roth, 1987
p. 236

目

I HOPE I HAVE it clear that the psychiatrist should avoid giving tacit consent to delusion or to very serious errors on the part of the patient. . . . In these cases, you should first confirm, by asking the most natural questions that would follow, that the patient intended to say what he did, and that there was no misunderstanding on your part. Having made sure that the patient's statement was as bad as it sounded—that he is entertaining an idea which is not only wrong, but also, in a sense, does violence to the possibility of his living in a social situation among others—you do not then say, "Oh, yes, yes. How interesting!" You rather say, "I can scarcely believe it. What on earth give you that impression?" You note a marked exception. . . . The patient is often quite grateful that I am not willing to go along at once with a marked misapprehension about something; although he may not be able to say it to me directly at the time, he, too, would like to get rid of these troublesome distortions. Always remember that no matter how sick a person is, the chances are that he is still more like you than he is different.

Harry Stack Sullivan, 1954
pp. 222–223

IN MY BRIEF experience, the most concise summary of treatment of the psychoses is Semrad's—help the patient to *acknowledge* (substitution of "real" affect for psychotic symptoms), *bear* (mourn with the patient, increase the ego's ability to bear anxiety and sadness), and *put his life into perspective* (working through one's feelings about one's abilities and disabilities as a person).

Sheldon Roth, 1970
pp. 57–58

WE CONSTANTLY aid these patients to see what formerly drove them crazy now makes them depressed.

Sheldon Roth, 1987
p. 172

EQUALLY DIFFICULT is the beginning of treatment with hebephrenics and paranoids, who are able but unwilling to verbalize. Here the tendency of the young therapist is to approach the patient with many questions in an attempt to make him talk. This attempt is understandable because there are many things that the therapist would like to know, and the therapist also tends to feel that if the patient is under pressure he will finally talk. However, from the point of view of therapy, this method should be discarded. Each question is experienced by the schizophrenic as an imposition or an intrusion into his private life and will increase his anxiety, his hostility, and his desire to desocialize. In certain respects the schizophrenic is like a young child. When a stranger visits a family and greets their young child by asking him questions, he will not be accepted by the child because the child feels that the stranger wants something from him. But later on, when the stranger is not a stranger any longer, if he asks questions that the child is capable of answering, the response will be favorable; contact will be made. The schizophrenic, too, in a later stage will be glad to answer questions that do not require an effort. In the beginning, however, no questions should be asked, because every question implies an effort. . . . The best procedure is to obtain as much information as possible from the members of the family, friends, or the doctor who first saw the patient.

Silvano Arieti, 1974
pp. 549–550

⊐

At the very beginning of treatment, when the patient's suspiciousness and distrust are very pronounced, he should leave the session with the feeling that he has been given something, not with the feeling that something, even diagnostic information, has been taken from him. When the patient has gained some security in contact with the therapist, he will talk more and more and eventually will even talk about his problems and give the therapist some historical material.

Silvano Arieti, 1974
pp. 550–551

⊐

If we do not ask questions, then what do we do with a withdrawn patient? As was mentioned in relation to catatonics, in the beginning the therapist takes the initiative and talks in a pleasant manner about neutral subjects.

Silvano Arieti, 1974
p. 550

Winnicott stated the problem simply and clearly when he said that psychoneurosis calls for classical analysis, but the inadequately mothered patient who has been disturbed from the beginning calls for management. Analysis in such cases, is, however, not ruled out or omitted. Whenever it proves feasible to do a bit of real analysis, it clarifies confused situations enormously. . . .

Harry Guntrip, 1971
p. 180

己

SUPPORTIVE PSYCHOTHERAPY

Supportive psychotherapy aims at reinforcing the defensive organization of the patient, tries to prevent the emergence of primitive transference paradigms, and tries to build up a working relationship in order to help the patient achieve more adaptive patterns of living.

Otto Kernberg, 1975
p. 71

己

. . . The therapist responds in ways which strengthen the patient's already existing defenses or introduce new defenses compatible with the existing overall defensive organization, in order to establish a more stable dynamic equilibrium. Examples include intellectualized interventions for patients who resort to isolation, encouragement of hobbies or other substitute activities for patients spontaneously embracing displacement, vacations for those with dependency needs, work and doing for others in patients employing reaction formations against dependency wishes, fostering new identifications, strengthening of rationalizations, etc.

Paul Dewald, 1976
p. 291

W HILE THE therapist encourages and supports the development of a . . . positive, trusting relationship, the focus of therapeutic attention is on the problems the patient has in situations outside of treatment. The therapist functions as a parent, a role model, a coach, an expert in human relations, and host of other helpful figures.

Gregory P. Bauer and Joseph Kobos, 1987
p. 269

TRANSFERENCE-INDUCED IMPROVEMENTS

. . . I F THE PATIENT is a "good boy" and does not behave neurotically, he gets love, protection, and "participation" from the omnipotent doctor; if he does not obey, he has to fear his revenge. In this respect, the psychotherapist is in good company: he uses the same means of influencing that God uses.

Otto Fenichel, 1945
p. 562

I N . . . INSIGHT-DIRECTED therapy, the attitude of the patient should come to be "speak first and think later," thereby fostering movement away from rigid adherence to the rules of the secondary process. . . . On the other hand, in supportive treatment strategy calls for the avoidance of further regression. Therefore, the therapist encourages the patient to an attitude expressed in the idea "think first and then speak," whereby he encourages the maintenance of the secondary process and strengthens the effectiveness of the ego defences.

Paul Dewald, 1964
pp. 166–167

EXPLORATORY VERSUS SUPPORTIVE THERAPY

O<small>NE CAN SAFELY</small> say that the use of either type of therapy when the other type is clearly indicated is bad therapy.

Jerome Kroll, 1988
p. 106

〓

W<small>E PROPOSE THAT</small> the psychiatric "suppressive-supportive" techniques are now outdated. . . . We think the correct dividing line is between analyzable and nonanalyzable structures. . . . Uncovering is not contraindicated in psychotherapy if the first therapeutic attention is to strengthening the ego to the point where it can tolerate "expressive-uncovering" techniques.

Gertrude and Rubin Blanck, 1974
p. 142

〓

E<small>GO SUPPORT</small> is probably one of the most mentioned and yet most misunderstood tools in psychotherapy. Some regard it simplistically as a "pat on the back" technique. "You did a good job," "You look well today," "You are a nice person," and the like . . . can be construed as ego support only if one abandons scientific definition of ego and uses it as has now become popular among laymen who refer to "ego boost" or "ego trip" when technically they mean narcissistic gratification. Of course, the patient's self-esteem is always to be maintained. But internalized, poor self-images do not yield to compliments.

Gertrude and Rubin Blanck, 1974
p. 345

〓

. . . C<small>AREFUL SAFEGUARDING</small> of autonomy is essential. . . . So-called supportive measures such as direct encouragement, advice, manipulation of the environment . . . all of which inevitably weaken the patient's capacity to cope with his own reality problems.

Gertrude and Rubin Blanck, 1974
p. 167

⊒

T HE EGO IS supported by searching out, diagnostically, those areas in which it has reached its highest points of development.

Gertrude and Rubin Blanck, 1974
p. 346

"B LANKET" SUPPORT such as "You are a courageous person," has little value unless it connects with a specific experience where the therapist can see how the ego functioned and can apprise the patient of it in *relation to that experience.*

Gertrude and Rubin Blanck, 1974
p. 346

⊒

A CCEPTANCE without the patient feeling that he is known by the analyst offers little comfort. The patient then feels he is accepted only because the analyst does not realize who he is as a person.

Allan Cooper and Earl Witenberg, 1983
p. 255

⊒

T HERE IS . . . nothing wrong with "supportive therapy" if "supportive" means taking the other person seriously and addressing oneself fully to the core of the patient's life situation and inner experience. Analysis to be fruitful must always be "supportive" in this sense of the term.

Erwin Singer, 1965
p. 347

T HERAPY IS therapy—talking to the patient about what matters to him, no matter at what pace he can take it.

Elvin Semrad, 1980
p. 102

12

The
Development
of a
Therapist

In a psychoanalytic session the other day, I controlled the impulse to remark, "When I was five and twenty, I heard a wise man say. . . ." A young man had come to consult me about two decisions that he had to make: should he follow a certain profession and ought he to marry a certain girl. Something in him or in his situation reminded me of myself at his age. he had just received his doctorate in psychology. I, too, had won my Ph.D. at this age and I was a student of Freud.

One evening I ran into the great man on his daily walk along the Ringstrasse in Vienna, and walked home with him. Friendly as always, he asked me about my plans and I told him of my problems, which resembled those of my present patient. Of course, I hoped Freud would give me advice or resolve my doubts.

"I can only tell you of my personal experience," he said. "When making a decision of minor importance, I have always found it advantageous to consider all the pros and cons. In vital matters, however, such as the choice of a mate of a profession, the decision should come from the unconscious, from somewhere within ourselves. In the important decisions of our personal life, we should be governed, I think, by the deep inner needs of our nature."

Without telling me what to do Freud had helped me make my own decision. Like marriage, the choice of a profession is a matter of destiny. We should welcome our destiny, readily accepting what comes with and out of it. On that evening thirty-five years ago when

I decided to become a psychoanalyst, I married the profession for better or for worse.

Theodor Reik, 1952
p. vii

⊒

THEORY

. . . ALL WORTHWHILE theorizing is tentative, probing, provisional— [it] contains an element of playfulness. I am using the word playfulness advisedly to contrast the basic attitude of creative science from that of dogmatic religion. The world of dogmatic religion, i.e., the world of absolute values, is serious; and those who live in it are serious because their joyful search has ended—they have become defenders of the truth. The world of creative science, however, is inhabited by playful people who understand that the reality that surrounds them is essentially unknowable. Realizing that they can never get at "the" truth, only at analogizing approximations, they are satisfied to describe what they see from various points of view and to explain it as best they can in a varity of ways.

Heinz Kohut, 1977
pp. 206–207

⊒

DESPITE THE polemics among various psychoanalytic theorists, there is much to learn from all of them. The appropriate question is not, Which theory is right? but rather, To what clinical issues can the therapist become more sensitive by understanding a given model? Much of the polarization among psychotherapists is a result of an emphasis on one factor and a relative neglect of others. Since patients can be understood from a number of points of view, a discussion of differences in emphasis is more helpful to the clinician than a debate about ultimate truth.

Andrew Druck, 1989
p. ix

MANY OF US like to learn only one trick. When this trick has its bad days, many of us become more insistent about its good days. We become devoted to a narrow school of practicing. . . . This is a shame. It is unfortunate for our patients, but even worse for ourselves. The richness of all the possible opposing currents becomes reduced to the same class of story over and over again. We lose connection with the fertility of the field. We stop learning. No one of these methods is worth the lifetime of a student. These teachers have already made that sacrifice. Therapists need a drift for their education which is good for a lifetime of curiosity and pleasure. Being locked in a snug harbor of dogmatism puts an end.

James Gustafson, 1986
p. 134

WHEN THEORIES are used as tools of observation, they have a properly limited half-life, which is determined by how long they maintain their heuristic and explanatory potential.

Paul and Anna Ornstein, 1985
p. 44

THEORY IS SIMPLY the best we can do to date to conceptualize the experiences our patients present to us.

Harry Guntrip, 1971
p. 21

TOO OFTEN theoretical concepts, which were meant merely as hypothetical constructs, become accepted as real and proven entities. . . . Theory may be a useful servant but it is a bad master.

Jules Bemporad, 1980
p. 57

Theory helps us make sense out of chaos; it helps us understand what is confusing on the surface and also points out the lacunae in our knowledge. It emphasizes what we do not know. . . . Psychotherapists who eschew theory have no such dilemma to face.

Peter Giovacchini, 1979
p. 12

⊐

LEARNING THE PSYCHOANALYTIC APPROACH

Anyone who hopes to learn the noble game of chess from books will soon discover that only the openings and end-games admit of an exhaustive systematic presentation and that the infinite variety of moves which develop after the opening defy any such description. This gap in instruction can only be filled by a diligent study of games fought out by masters. The rules which can be laid down for the practice of psycho-analytic treatment are subject to similar limitations.

Sigmund Freud, 1913
p. 123

⊐

I think I am well-advised, however, to call these rules "recommendations" and not to claim any unconditional acceptance for them. The extraordinary diversity of the psychical constellations concerned, the plasticity of all mental processes and the wealth of determining factors oppose any mechanization of the technique

Sigmund Freud, 1913
p. 123

⊐

Freud was admittedly and intentionally rather restrained in formulating technical rules; and we are still far from dispensing a collection

of technical prescriptions that would cover every given situation. . . .
In teaching one must avoid giving the student the impression that
actually a complete set of rules exists which just his lack of experience
prevents him from knowing.

Heinz Hartmann, 1951
pp. 32–33

⊒

. . . T HE "ONTOGENETIC development" of the individual therapist to
some extent recapitulates the "Phylogenetic development" of psychoanalysis. Freud and the early workers were at first particularly preoccupied with the various dramatic, insistent and compelling manifestations of the drives and their derivatives. it was only after continuing
and more sophisticated clinical experience that their attention was
increasingly focused on the other components of mental life. It was
this shift which resulted in the development of the structural hypoth-
esis and an increasing emphasis on ego and super-ego psychology. This
same evolution occurs during the training and development of most
dynamic psychiatrists. Initially their attention and interest is directed
towards verifying the presence of the unconscious drives and their
various manifest derivatives. It is only after increased clinical experience that they develop a corresponding interest in ego and super-ego
functions, and recognize their importance as determinants of psychopathology.

Paul Dewald, 1964
p. 189

⊒

IT IS WORTH reminding the reader that Semrad used to remark on the
learning pattern of the serious psychotherapist: Ontogeny recapitulates phylogeny. . . . Therapists who undergo psychoanaltyic training
often find that the constraints of classical analysis, which are appropriate for the situations for which they are designed, begin to be used
with nonpsychoanalytic patients. The neutral-mirror simile . . . takes

over their technique. Like many analysts of earlier generations, they may take years to retrace their intuitive steps toward the creative use of spontaneous and empathic countertransferences.

Sheldon Roth, 1987
p. 82

⊐

EXPERIENCE is a tricky factor to consider. I think it was Sartre who said somewhere that experience usually consists of somebody's repeating the same errors over a long enough period to feel entitled to claim some absolute authority for doing things in that faulty way.

Roy Schafer, 1983
p. 287

⊐

THE NEOPHYTE therapist, as well as the experienced one, is often stunned by the extent of the hostility with which good intentions are met. If any one element is underestimated in approaching a career as a psychotherapist, it is the amount of hostility and rejection that will be one's lot in the pursuit of therapeutic helpfulness. A great threat to personal integrity and self-worth will come about through open rejection of one's most heartfelt efforts to be of use, the sharing of intuitions with the patient, and the provision of great patience and forbearance; the patient may still, in spite of all these, declare the therapist inadequate, short of the mark, and uncaring.

Sheldon Roth, 1987
pp. 1–2

⊐

LEST HE LOSE the independence required for his work, it is important for the beginning therapist to realize that his concept of himself must not depend on the patient's evaluation of the outcome of the therapists' efforts. If a therapist operates out of concern about what the patient, his relatives, and the community at large will think of him in a given situation, he cannot help but be influenced by irrelevant considerations; he will end up working to win love and admiration instead of single-mindedly striving toward the legitimate goal of insight psychotherapy: promoting the patient's increased understanding of his or her own character and its motivations.

Michael Basch, 1980
p. 62

THERE ARE TWO kinds of feelings that patients display toward the therapist that are avoided by the neophyte. First, there is the reality response of anger or annoyance on the part of the patient as being misunderstood; this can be unsettling to a beginning therapist. But these feelings are not too different from similar feelings toward physicians in other specialties of medicine. Second—and this is new and different—is the transference that develops, Although beginning therapists are given an intellectual awareness of transference, it is most difficult to describe before the fact. The dependent, hostile, and/or erotic feelings patients develop in the psychotherapy situation must be experienced firsthand.

Gerald Roskin and Charles Rabiner, 1976
p. 327

I HAVE BEEN teaching and training young analysts for many years and I know that nothing is more difficult for them than to control their impatience. The temptation to help quickly and—what must necessarily precede every therapeutic effort—to understand quickly, is a strong one for the inexperienced. Looking back upon my own early analytic work, I realize how impatient I was myself, how ready to form judgments and to make premature interpretations, how hasty sometimes in my conclusion.

Theodor Reik, 1952
p. 127

THE MAJOR TASK of the maturing therapist is to learn to tolerate uncertainty.

Irvin Yalom, 1980
p. 410

SUPERVISION

SULLIVAN'S statement (quoted by Levenson, 1982) "God keep me from a therapy that goes well!" can be extended to "Keep me from a supervisory relationship that goes well!" *Going well* may mean that there is more superficiality in the relationship but less anxiety; a more comfortable atmosphere but limited interpersonal engagement; a greater sense of certainty but complexities are dissociated; more interpretations but little structural change in the relatedness between participants; more efforts to preserve the status quo but less opportunities for experiencing new dimensions of oneself and the other; that disappointments and struggles have more likely been avoided, but the potential richness and joy of a significant relationship is lost.

Ruth Lessor, 1984
p. 151

. . . THE BEST SUPERVISORS are those who students do not remember as being particularly clever, because they experienced their own growing effectiveness as the heart of the process.

Phillip Bromberg, 1984
p. 36

SELF-DISCLOSURE and self-scrutiny in the presence of another person does arouse some anxiety. The student is most often quite able to handle his own self-esteem needs provided that the setting encourages activity and give-and-take between the two participants. This includes questioning and disagreeing, comparing the supervisor's opinion and perspective with his own, freedom to comment in an ongoing way on the supervisory process itself and the supervisor's impact, and in general, an atmosphere that encourages self-regulation rather than passive ingestion.

Phillip Bromberg, 1984
pp. 35–36

Though the parallel process may at times be a small or a large part of the supervisory relationship, it is always there. When the supervisor and student analyst are not aware of it, a glorious learning opportunity is missed. When the parallel process is not recognized, there is the danger that what transpires will be understood solely in terms of transference and countertransference. The analyst-supervisor relationship may then deteriorate in the same way as did the patient–analyst relationship — an unaware parallel processing is going on with the therapist and the supervisor bending to the contours of the patient's pathology.

Leopold Caligor, 1981
p. 22

The reality and value of maintaining traditional distinctions between the psychoanalytic and the supervisory situations are questionable. Many presumed differences prove to be illusory and probably serve defensive purposes. If anxieties inherent in the supervisory situation are not appreciated, they may interfere with the goals of supervision.

Ruth Lessor, 1984
p. 144

To STATE THE matter in extreme terms, everybody appears to oppose "treatment" of the supervisee, and yet everybody does it. Some do it with misgivings, and some without.

Daryl Debell, 1981
p. 42

己

HYPERINTELLECTUALISM and lack of empathy seem to go hand in hand. The principal problem of the overempathic resident is overidentification with the patient. There is an important distinction between empathy and identification. Empathy facilitates treatment: identification paralyzes it. When there are administrative difficulties I generally suspect paranoid problems, though it need not always be so.

Sidney Tarachow, 1963
p. 308

THE THERAPIST is permitted to have neurotic problems of character — they may actually be desirable — but they must be of a nature that does not limit the therapist's further growth and development. Excessive sadism, inability to profit from life despite earlier neurotic difficulties, and rigidity of defenses based on anxiety arising from challenges to narcissistic issues (such as infantile omnipotence) are some of the foremost barriers to becoming an effective therapist. Persons with substantial components of these factors should consider another profession.

Sheldon Roth, 1987
p. 8

己

IN SOME INSTANCES, where I have found a complex of factors which seemed to me to preclude a successful career in psychiatry, among them some grievous disorder of personality, I have disadvised the pursuit of the career on the basis of my impression of its unsuitability to the person—but only *after* I had uncovered some interest in an alternative course, *and* some of the experience that had eventuated in the "choice" of psychiatry. By virtue of questioning the validity of the "choice" and recommending reconsideration I have spared us both embarrassment about the actual personal problems. The tendency towards mental health does the rest, with no danger of serious disturbance to the candidate.

Harry Stack Sullivan, 1947
pp. 214–215

〺

THERAPY FOR THERAPISTS

No ONE WHO, like me, conjures up the most evil of those half-tamed demons that inhabit the human breast, and seeks to wrestle with them can expect to come through the struggle unscathed.

Sigmund Freud, 1905a
p. 109

〺

A THERAPIST IS an entirely human therapeutic instrument and, as such, is heir to all the frailties of the human condition. Personal neglect and denial can only diminish one's therapeutic effectiveness.

Sheldon Roth, 1987
p. 25

〺

EVERY ANALYST ought periodically himself to submit to analysis, at intervals of, say, five years, without any feeling of shame in so doing. This is as much as to say that not only the patient's analysis but that of the analyst himself is a task which is never finished.

Sigmund Freud, 1937
p. 402

IT IS CLEAR that personal therapy is necessary to help us, as therapists, try to resolve what is resolvable, make as clear as possible what our psychological blind spots are and which personal scars are intractable, and familiarize ourselves with the slipperiness of the unconscious.

Sheldon Roth, 1987
p. 8

ᗕ

THE TRAINING-ANALYSIS has accomplished its purpose if it imparts to the novice a sincere conviction of the existence of the unconscious, enables him through the emergence of repressed material in his own mind to perceive in himself processes which otherwise he would have regarded as incredible and gives him a first sample of the technique which has proved to be the only correct method in conducting analyses.

Sigmund Freud, 1937
p. 401

ᗕ

THE AIM OF the analyst's own analysis . . . is not to turn him into a mechanical brain which can produce interpretations on the basis of a purely intellectual procedure, but to enable him, to *sustain* the feelings which are stirred in him as opposed to discharging them (as does the patient), in order to *subordinate* them to the analytic task in which he functions as the patient's mirror reflection.

Paula Heimann, 1950
p. 82

ᗕ

THROUGHOUT the inception of the interview, the psychiatrist. . . should know how he acts — that is, he should have learned from experience the usual impression obtained of him in the particular circumstance of encountering the sort of stranger that the interviewer at first glance seems to be.

Harry Stack Sullivan, 1954
p. 63

⊒

. . . EACH PSYCHOTHERAPIST brings to his work his own equipment which he uses every day with other people, some of it for good and some for ill. The problem for every psychotherapist is to sort out the things he does well with others and try to build up his psychotherapeutic armament out of those.

Harry Stack Sullivan, 1954
p. 213

⊒

I MUST HOWEVER make it clear that what I am asserting is that this technique is the only one suited to my individuality; I do not venture to deny that a physician quite differently constituted might find himself driven to adopt a different attitude to his patients and to the tasks before him.

Sigmund Freud, 1912b
p. 111

⊒

NOBODY CAN analyze every type of analysand. . . . There are certain types of empathizing and certain types of situations that are simply not your cup of tea. No one is to be blamed, really.

Roy Schafer, 1983
pp. 290–291

T HE TIME IS likely to come when you ask yourself, "To whom would I refer someone I love?" or "To whom would I go for a second analysis?"

Roy Schafer, 1983
p. 28

13

Growing Up

THE ONLY THING that the child cannot do for himself is to give himself a basic sense of security; . . that is a function of object-relationship.

Harry Guntrip, 1969
p. 193

⊒

. . . THE IMPORTANCE of security for babies and mother outweighs every other issue . . . . The mother's ability to give her baby a secure start in life "does not depend on knowledge but on a feeling" that comes naturally if she herself feels secure.

Harry Guntrip, 1971
p. 114

⊒

THE PARENTS' responsibility is not to mold, shape, pattern or condition him, but to support him in such a way that his precious hidden uniqueness shall be able to emerge and guide his whole development.

Harry Guntrip, 1971
p. 181

YOU RECALL Freud's dictum to the effect that it is the parents' superego, not their ego, that is communicated to the unconscious of the child; not what parents would like the child to believe but what they unconsciously do believe.

Michael Basch, 1985
p. 35

⊐

MY POINT IS that human happiness is not determined by breast feeding, leisurely toilet training, or the absence of childhood surgery. As Erikson has written, children need to be patiently taught basic trust, automony, initiative—then adult games, friends, vacations, and social supports may follow.

George Valiant, 1977
p. 295

⊐

PERHAPS THE most important thing Fairbairn ever wrote was that the cause of mental illness lay in the fact that "parents fail to get it across to the child that he is loved for his own sake, as a person in his own right."

Harry Guntrip, 1971
p. 112

⊐

OPTIMAL FRUSTRATION

AN IMPORTANT function of the material object is to regulate the frustrations of the critical periods; not to remove frustration, but, when necessary, to impose it, for optimal frustration is structure (and ego) building.

Gertrude and Rubin Blanck, 1974
p. 50

IN A GOOD holding environment, minor failures in the mother's or the therapist's empathy are unavoidable, and lead the baby or the patient to absorb gradually and silently that which the mother or therapist used to do for the baby or patient.

Richard Chessick, 1985
p. 118

... WITH EACH OF the mother's minor empathic failures, misunder-standings, and delays, the infant withdraws narcissistic libido from the archaic image of unconditional perfection (primary narcissism) and acquires in its stead a particle of inner psychological structure which takes over the mother's functions in the service of the maintenance of narcissistic equilibrium, e.g., her basic soothing and calming activities; and her providing physical and emotional warmth and other kinds of narcissistic sustenance. Thus, as continues to hold true for the anal-ogous later millieu of the child, the most important aspect of the earliest mother–infant ralationship is the principle of optimal frustration.

Heinz Kohut, 1971
p. 64

... GOOD MOTHERING ... imposes just enough frustration to help the ego develop, but no more.

Gertrude and Rubin Blanck, 1974
p. 223

IF ALL GOES *well* the infant can actually come to gain from the experience of frustration, since incomplete adapatation to need makes objects real, that is to say hated as well as loved.

D. W. Winnicott, 1953
p. 94

... A MODICUM OF frustration of the child's trust in the self-object's empathic perfection is necessary, not only in order to usher in transmuting internalizations which build up the structures necessary for the tolerance of delays, but also in order to stimulate the acquisition of responses that are in harmony with the fact that the world contains real enemies, i.e., other selves whose narcissistic requirements run counter to the survival of one's own self.

Heinz Kohut, 1977
p. 123

ᔎ

OPPOSITIONALISM and negativism, so often viewed solely as resistance based upon the defense of reaction formation, can also represent a struggle to establish and maintain identity. To be sure, this, too, may be a defense, in this instance against symbiotic wishes; on the other hand it may also be seen as a normal step toward separation–individuation.

Gertrude and Rubin Blanck, 1974
p. 195

ᔎ

... CHILDREN MUST have discipline. It helps them overcome the fear of their own aggression and to regain control of their own aggression.

Sidney Tarachow, 1963
p. 90

ᔎ

THE TRANSITIONAL OBJECT

THE TOY THAT mother has given him comes to his rescue if he becomes anxious. It reminds him of her, stands for her and her reliability, and keeps alive his mental image of her until she comes back in time to reassure his personally.

Harry Guntrip, 1971
p. 119

◲

... T HE CHILD MUST organize his world of reality long before he can reason as adults reason.

Norman Cameron, 1963
p. 610

◲

T HESE INCORPORATED early parental images, which form the nucleus of unconscious super-ego function, do not necessarily reflect parental attitudes and standards as they actually occurred, but rather are an internalization of the child's perception, anticipation and interpretation of the parents' attitudes.

Paul Dewald, 1964
p. 10

◲

T HE THING TO remember is that a small child will represent an experience to himself—symbolize it in his imagery—not as it would have appeared in a moving picture with a sound track, but as he himself experienced it, with all the small child misinterpretations, misunderstandings, ambivalent feelings, omissions, passions and distortions intact.

Norman Cameron, 1963
p. 203

I<small>T IS NOT</small> only inevitable. It is also essential that a child develop the *grand illusion* of one day marrying a parent and, after a painful struggle, experience the tragedy of having to give it up. This is the natural human way for little boys to prepare to grow into men who can love women, and for little girls to prepare to grow into women who can love men.

Norman Cameron, 1963
p. 69

T<small>HE NEED THAT</small> every infant and child normally has to be led, guided and controlled by a loving parent may persist in its original form, especially if one's parents are unusually possessive. . . . We often see adults who remain in the parental home, usually unmarried, and sometimes quite contented with their dependence. A persistent need for parental love may be strong enough to cause failure if the dependent person does marry. It is sometimes a factor in creating the Don Juans and the seductive, dissatisfied women who never succeed in finding among their contemporaries the kind of love they want. It is likewise a factor in producing chronically infantile adults who seek, and occasionally find, a repetition in their marriage of the dependent relationship which they never resolved in childhood.

Norman Cameron, 1963
p. 118

O<small>PTIMAL PARENTS</small>—again I should rather say: optimally failing parents—are people who, despite their stimulation by and competition with the rising generation, are also sufficiently in touch with the pulse of life, accept themselves sufficiently as transient participants in the ongoing stream of life, to be able to experience the growth of the next generation with unforced nondefensive joy.

Heinz Kohut, 1977
p. 237

CHILDREN WHO have been loved do not require disguises which are that difficult to read. They have confidence in being found out.

James Gustafson, 1986
p. 18

IDENTIFICATION AND CHARACTER FORMATION

... THE CHILD TAKES on the archaically construed characters of both parents and then is faced with the life-long problem of reconciling these components. Other figures may also be involved, of course, such as siblings or other relatives. This problem of reconciliation is all the more difficult when the parents are deeply at odds with one another or severely conflict-ridden in their own right, or, as is so often the case, both.

Roy Schafer, 1983
p. 149

IN MY OPINION, the most common cause of sexual or gender uncertainty is the fact that the child who feels rejected by both parents tends also to reject both parents and therefore has difficulties in identifying with either one of them.

Silvano Arieti, 1974
p. 93

THE NORMAL CHILD replaces most of his oedipal curiosity with a general curiosity, an eagerness to learn, which he retains for most of his lifetime.

Norman Cameron, 1963
p. 82

EXPERIENCES OF mastery, with sympathetic adult help, are among the best of early preparations for independent mastery.

Norman Cameron, 1963
p. 124

◫

WITH PREADOLESCENCE, the capacity to care for the happiness of someone else as much as for one's own appears for the first time, and Sullivan considers this the most important period in terms of acculturation. If the child does not succeed at this period in forming a close bond with a contemporary, he will go through life isolated and gravely handicapped.

Clara Thompson, 1952
p. 109

◫

A TEN-YEAR-OLD is often better integrated than his adolescent counterpart.

George Valiant, 1977
p. 210

◫

OVER AND OVER again, in early development, libido will seek connection while aggression will seek and maintain separation and individuation. In adolescence, the separating needs are served by still another temporary phase-dominant aggressive thrust, to be followed by libidinally powered search for connection with a new, contemporary object.

Gertrude and Rubin Blanck, 1979
p. 39

Autonomy precedes intimacy and is simpler to achieve than intimacy since the latter involves the constant exposure to fears of abandonment and/or engulfment.

James Masterson, 1976
p. 174

🔁

The entrance to the adult life cycle is through the portal of adolescence. . . . Identity formation in adolescence is fostered by a curious fact of human nature; as we lose or separate ourselves from people that we love, we internalize them. Thus, as adolescents turn to communes, to a college-on-the-opposite-coast, as adolescents consciously focus on all that is bad about their parents in order to extricate themselves from the backwards pull, they escape and take their parents with them.

George Valiant, 1977
p. 207

🔁

. . . A stormy adolescence per se is no obstacle to normal adult maturation. In fact, it often bodes well.

George Valiant, 1977
p. 207

🔁

What happens to those who grow up in tormented, highly conflicted families? One might expect that they would kick up their heels with joy at the prospect of dancing away from such a family. But the opposite occurs: the more disturbed the family, the harder it is for progeny to leave: they are ill equipped to separate, and cling to the family. . . .

Irvin Yalom, 1980
p. 399

T HE ONLY TIME people leave their mothers is when they're ready to go.

Elvin Semrad, 1980
p. 53

己

T HE MOST BASIC temptation between two individuals is the urge to regress in the character of object relations and to dissolve boundaries and fuse. Normal sexual intercourse offers just such an opportunity. Identification and object relations are not too far removed from symbiotic feelings and are an attempt to restore the symbiotic feelings. . . . It is a paradox that object relations, which we take as a mark of reality adjustment, are really designed to circumvent the painful recognition of reality.

Sidney Tarachow, 1963
p. 16

己

T HE CHILD WANTS to do what the adult does, and the adult wants to do what the child does.

Sidney Tarachow, 1963
p. 55

己

A T EVERY STEP of development, some degree of sadness requires acknowledgment, bearing, and being put into place. The toddler often needs to run back to its mother for "emotional refueling." Going off to kindergarten, completion of schooling, getting married, and forming one's own family all entail loss of cherished places and people. It is commonplace to cry at weddings and occasions of great happiness.

Sheldon Roth, 1987
p. 144

ONE CANNOT proceed with the next stage of development without proper mourning of the last.

Sheldon Roth, 1987
p. 143

IT WAS HARD to tell what stunted the growth of this man. My guess— and it is no more than a guess—is that we stop growing when our human losses are no longer replaced. . . . The seeds of love must be eternally resown.

George Valiant, 1977
p. 210

IF ONE IS to love oneself one must behave in ways that one can admire.

Irvin Yalom, 1980
p. 334

EACH OF AN individual's relationships reflects the others: it is rare, I believe, for one to be able to relate in bad faith to some individuals and in an authentic, caring way to a select few.

Irvin Yalom, 1980
p. 390-

W HEN TREATING A patient who has difficulty establishing an enduring relationship, it is always rewarding for the therapist to inquire deeply about the texture of the patient's other, less intense relationships. Love problems are not situation-specific. Love is not a specific encounter but an attitude. A problem of not-being-loved is more often than not a problem of not loving.

Irvin Yalom, 1980
p. 377

O NE, AFTER ALL, does not *find* a relationship; one forms a relationship

Irvin Yalom, 1980
p. 387

S OME FRENCH *philosophe* has penned an aphorism that every woman gets the husband she deserves. Analytically this could be rephrased to the effect that every woman gets the husband for whom she is emotionally ready.

Reuben Fine, 1979
p. 143

T HE MOST IMPORTANT function of a human being is to make up his mind what's for him and what's not for him

Elvin Semrad, 1980
p. 15

RESIDENT: He [the patient] told me that although his early experiences with sex were exclusively with prostitutes, he had thought when he got married that that would no longer be the case. However, he found that his wife wasn't really much interested in sexual play, and that she resented his attempts to make their relationship more passionate. When they learned that they couldn't have children because he was sterile, his wife rapidly lost what interest she had demonstrated in the sexual aspect of marriage. It became clear to him, he says, without it ever being openly discussed, that she preferred that he take his sexual needs elsewhere to be fulfilled. It was just a matter of time before he fell back into his old pattern of seeking out prostitutes.

I still couldn't believe that that was all there was to it, so I asked him if he didn't feel to some extent conscience-stricken or guilty about it. . . . It was as if with that question we shifted roles. I thought Mr. C. might get mad or defensive. Instead, he became positively avuncular. He settled back in his chair, gave me a long, kindly look, and said, in effect, that I had helped him a lot and was obviously far more educated than he, but, meaning no disrespect, in these matters his having lived longer put him in the position of perhaps teaching me something. He then told me, in essence, that he and his wife had had a very good life together, and that their marriage was an affectionate and mutually sustaining one which, he felt, it would not have been if he had continued to make an issue out of their sex life. As a young man he, too, had had an idealized concept of how life should be lived, but he found that those people he knew who couldn't compromise their picture of what things should be like tended to end up with nothing, while he and those he knew who accepted disappointment gracefully and worked around it as best they could tended to end up reasonably happy. No, he said, he wasn't guilty or upset about his weekly excursions to the house he and his friends visited. Perhaps with the years, I, too, would be more understanding of how little that meant when weighed against the totality of a relationship. What had bothered him so much more for a number of years was the absence of children.

Michael Basch, 1980
pp. 102–103

... L IFE DEMANDS compromises and half-solutions.

Theodor Reik, 1952
p. 235

W HEN CAN A man be his own man? Only when he can be honest and discreet with his old man.

Elvin Semrad, 1980
p. 42

M OST OF US do not know what we really want.

Ernst Beier, 1966
p. 123

T HE NEED FOR definite ego boundaries in normal object relations has been vastly overestimated. Healthy object relations permit and even demand periodic regressions and fusions, for example, carnivals, vacations, religious belief, love-making. Schizophrenics show the most brittle and rigid ego boundaries of all.

Sidney Tarachow, 1963
p. 16

Nobody ever thinks *too* much.

Elvin Semrad, 1980
p. 71

We are all wrestling with the same emotional problems, and it is often only a matter of proportion that determines whether we are victorious or defeated.

Theodor Reik, 1952
p. 59

In most general terms, we are all much more simply human than otherwise, be we happy and successful, contented and detached, miserable and mentally disordered, or whatever.

Harry Stack Sullivan, 1947
p. 16

14

Psychodynamics

ACCORDING TO legend King Phylacus had a son Iphiclus who was impotent. The king said to Melampus, "I will grant you your freedom and some first-rate cattle if you will only cure my son of impotence." Melampus agreed and began the task by sacrificing two bulls to Apollo. After he had burned the thigh bones with the fat, he left their carcasses lying by the alter. Presently two vultures arrived, and one said to the other, "It must be several years since we were last here—that time when Phylacus was gelding rams and we collected our perquisites."

"I well remember it," said the other vulture. "Iphiclus, who was then still a child, saw his father coming toward him with a blood-stained knife and took fright. He apparently feared to be gelded himself, because he screamed at the top of his voice. Phylacus drove the knife into the sacred pear tree over there for safe-keeping, while he ran to comfort Iphiclus. That fright accounts for the impotency. And Phylacus forgot to recover the knife! There it still is, sticking in the tree. But bark has grown over its blade, and only the end of its handle shows."

"In that case," remarked the first vulture, "the remedy for Iphiclus's impotence would be to draw out the knife, scrape off the rust left by the rams' blood, and administer it to him, mixed in water, every day for ten days." Needless to say, this remedy worked.

Richard Chessick, 1974
p. 5

253

FREUD ... HAS provided an image of man that has made him comprehensible without at the same time making him contemptible.

Jerome Brunner, 1957
p. 285

⊐

IN THE AREA of psychodynamics common sense is a treacherous guide, by whom we may be led through familiar paths to turn a corner and suddenly find our guide and ourselves totally lost.

David Malan, 1979
p. 44

⊐

IN PSYCHOANALYTIC relations things often happen differently from what the psychology of consciousness might lead us to expect.

Sigmund Freud, 1912b
p. 118

⊐

THIS THERAPY, then, is based on the recognition that unconscious ideas—or better, the unconsciousness of certain mental processes—are the direct cause of the morbid symptoms.

Sigmund Freud, 1905b
p. 266

W E OFTEN HEAR patients complain that they fail to concentrate their attention. In analytic investigation we find that this complaint conceals a totally different situation. The attention of these patients is concentrated, though, upon an unconscious content, for instance, certain fantasies. They fail to detach attention from particular psychical contents and direct it to others, which is what life demands of them.

Theodor Reik, 1952
p. 169

己

T HE ANALYST'S work is to see the unconscious in action.

Ella Freeman Sharpe, 1930
p. 21

己

T HE UNDERSTANDING of symbols as expressive rather than repressive has important practical consequences. It allows for the insight that symptoms are the patient's representations of his inner state. The symptom a patient exhibits is then an expression, symbolic as any expression must be, of his inner situation.

Erwin Singer, 1965
p. 84

己

M ENTAL LIFE IS not a homogeneous stream flowing serene and unruffled, without crosscurrents, eddies, and backwaters. On the contrary, to switch metaphors in mid-stream, it has many aspects of a house divided against itself.

John C. Nemiah, 1973
p. 35

Essentially, psychoanalysis is a psychology of conflict.

Jacob Arlow, 1980
p. 193

PSYCHIC DETERMINISM

All human behavior is . . . the purposeful product of an interaction between internal psychic forces and the forces and limitations of external reality. There are no irrelevant, meaningless, or purposeless thoughts, dreams, or acts.

Richard Chessick, 1974
p. 25

Nothing in mental life occur in a random or unselected fashion. . . .

Paul Dewald, 1964
p. 41

The qualities conscious, preconscious or unconscious as applied to mental phenomena may be considered to exist on a continuum. Each may be seen as zonal, with gradations within the zone, and with no sharp dividing line between them.

Paul Dewald, 1964
p. 5

T HE REALM OF the unconscious appears to have a timelessness about it that is absent in our ordinary consciousness, where memories fade and pale.

John C. Nemiah, 1973
p. 63

◻

A N EVENT IN later life that has affinities with . . . buried, unresolved childhood conflict tends to activate and bring into consciousness the old, unconscious feelings and fantasies and impulses that were never laid to rest in the earlier years of development.

John C. Nemiah, 1973
p. 81

◻

I N THE UNCONSCIOUS, the repressed seems to flourish . . . like the hidden roots of a tree.

Norman Cameron, 1963
p. 192

◻

I T IS TRUE that unconscious, infantile strivings enter into the motivation of most thoughts and acts; but this does not mean that the unconscious, infantile contributions always reveal a person's dominant motives. The unconscious drive may be only a parasitic rider.

Norman Cameron, 1963
p. 141

. . . W HEN THE MIND evolves into a more mature mode of operation, the earlier mode does not disappear, but rather succumbs to the dominance of the newer form, always ready and able to reemerge in the appropriate situation.

Thomas Paolino, 1981
p. 81

॒

B EHIND ALL ACTIVE types of mastery of external and internal tasks, a readiness remains to fall back to passive-receptive types of mastery. . . . In mental development, earlier levels still persist along with or underneath higher levels.

Otto Fenichel, 1945
p. 53

॒

REPETITION COMPULSION

T HE PATIENT SEEKS to repeat previous experiences of psychic importance, either to achieve again the pleasure of those infantile and childhood drives which were gratified, or to re-experience previously frustrating situations with the goal of achieving gratification this time.

Paul Dewald, 1964
p. 195

॒

T HE NEED TO repeat is predicated on the fact that we have an inner set of fantasies as to what life is, what mother is, what father is, what love is, what disappointment is. In a certain sense we cannot act outside the limits of those fantasies. We relentlessly proceed to create a life which conforms to those fantasies.

Sidney Tarachow, 1963
p. 199

... T<small>HE EGO CONTINUALLY</small> scans the reality situation seeking for objects on which to displace or project the drives and drive-derivatives, or for use in the defence against the drives. The stronger the unconscious drive which is seeking gratification, or the more intense the defence against such a drive, the greater will be the need to make this type of neurotic object choice in the external world. When such objects are available, the individual will tend to become repetitively involved with them in a stereotyped fashion.

Paul Dewald, 1964
p. 70

A<small>T FIRST GLANCE</small> it seems as though neurotic patients get into anxiety-provoking situations wholly by accident. A careful study of the life situations of the patient ... reveal quite a different picture. Chance does play a part, of course, as it does in the mishaps of everyone. But in addition we find that certain conflictual situations attract these individuals, possess a special fascination for them, of which they are nearly always unaware. They are unconsciously preoccupied with unresolved conflicts, and this preoccupation pushes them into situations that allow their conflicts some degree of expression. In fact, they themselves often help to create such situations out of whatever interpersonal relationships present themselves. ...

Norman Cameron, 1963
p. 266

P<small>ATIENTS ALMOST</small> regularly project superego functions into the analyst and then react as if they are being judged.

Peter Giovacchini, 1979
p. 449

IF THERE IS a valid and real attitude toward the self, that attitude will manifest as valid and real toward others. It is not that ye judge so shall ye be judged, but as you judge yourself so shall you judge others; strange but true as far as I know, and with no exception.

Harry Stack Sullivan, 1947
p. 15

PATIENTS WITH primitive mental state often try to create a setting where their projections need not be viewed as projections. That is, they attempt to induce in the therapist feelings and behaviors which are consistent with their view of themselves and of the interpersonal environment.

Althea Horner, 1980
p. 198

THE MORE THAT object choice in the environment is based on unconscious intra-psychic conflict, or attempts at conflict resolution, the greater will be the potentialities for disruption and disturbance in external relationships.

Paul Dewald, 1964
p. 71

IN ESSENCE, THEN, what happened was that D. . . had certain beliefs about men, certain expectancies about how they would behave toward her. These expectancies distorted her perception, and perceptual distortion resulted in her behaving in ways *that elicited the very behavior she dreaded.* This maneuver, the "self-fulfilling prophecy," is common:

the individual first expects a certain event to occur, then behaves in such a way as to bring the prophecy to pass, and finally *relegates awareness of his or her behavior to the unconscious.*

Irvin Yalom, 1980
p. 235

凸

W E THINK WE leave childhood behind us, but how we look at the world when we are adults is very much tied to the way the world looked to us then.

Michael Basch, 1980
p. 44

凸

T HE UNLOVED often have a special capacity to identify and to empathize with the pain and suffering in the world.

George Valiant, 1977
p. 294

凸

SEX

T HERE WAS a time when a typical misunderstanding of the implications of psychoanalytic theory and practice was the assumption that sexual activity in itself was a therapeutic factor. We have advanced a long way from such misunderstandings, and have learned that often what appears on the surface to be genital activity is actually in the service of . . . pregenital aims.

Otto Kernberg, 1975
p. 103

THOSE WHO cannot make genuinely personal relations often fall back on bodily sexual relations as a substitute, only to find that sex does not fill the aching mental void.

Harry Guntrip, 1971
p. 36

ⅎ

DEPENDENCY

IN GENERAL, "excessive dependency" usually turns out to reflect an internal incapacity to really depend upon others and on what is received from them.

Otto Kernberg, 1975
p. 202

ⅎ

AGGRESSION

AGGRESSION IS A defensive reaction of a threatened ego.

Harry Guntrip, 1971
p. 84

ⅎ

. . . EXCESSIVE unneutralized aggression forestalls comfortable use of the aggressive drive in the service of separation.

Gertrude and Rubin Blanck, 1974
p. 244

W E DO NOT seek to rid a patient of aggression because it is "wrong" or "negative," but only because, in unneutralized form, it is not available to the ego for purposes that serve the patient.

Gertrude and Rubin Blanck, 1974
p. 273

⊒

I NITIATIVE, enterprise and regulated competition are all common expressions of primitive aggression that has been tamed by ego action, and is available for activities which may be energetically constructive or creative.

Norman Cameron, 1963
p. 180

⊒

O NE OF THE greatest siphoners of aggression . . . is work.

Emil Gutheil, 1959
p. 805

⊒

I T IS MORE tolerable for the child to think that he is punished by the good parent because he deserves to be punished than to think that he unfairly punished. If he is punished although he is not bad, he will have a feeling of despair; the situation will seem to him beyond remedy, hopeless. . . . Some children actually force themselves to do "bad things" in order to be bad because they want to be punished for something that they have done rather than for nothing.

Silvano Arieti, 1974
p. 95

IT IS MORE bearable to feel hated for what one *does* than for what one *is*.

Frieda Fromm-Reichmann, 1950
p. 53

FEAR AND GUILT are both object-relations. . . . In the end human beings prefer bad relationships to none at all.

Harry Guntrip, 1969
p. 202

SHE WAS AN adult before her time, and as an adult she sheds the responsibility of adulthood.

William Mueller and Albert Aniskiewicz, 1986
p. 79

THERE ARE FIGHTING phobias, seen in persons who become frightened whenever aggressive behavior would be indicated. For such cases, a formula is valid which would be an oversimplification in more complicated cases: what a person fears, he unconsciously wishes for.

Otto Fenichel, 1945
p. 196

THE REACTIONS of feeling sorry, appreciative, or frightened were expected by the parent and produced by the child in order to gain parental approval. Later, these same processes operated intrapsychically as the ego attempted to obtain approval from internalized objects.

Roger Mackinnon and Robert Michels, 1971
p. 139

〓

... THIS INTERNAL world of object representations as seen in conscious, preconscious, and unconscious fantasies never reproduces the *actual* world of real people with whom the individual has established relationships in the past and in the present; it is at most an approximation, always strongly influenced by the very early object-images of introjections and identifications.

Otto Kernberg, 1976
p. 33

〓

BY PROVOCATION, seduction, ingratiation, and confession, the environment is drawn into the conflict between the ego and the superego, in the hope of obtaining some relief. Much of what is called object relationships are actually pseudo object relationships, in which the subject does not develop any feelings toward the object as a person but uses the object as an instrument for achieving relief in a conflict with his superego.

Otto Fenichel, 1945
p. 166

〓

MASOCHISM

PATIENTS WILL OFTEN provoke you to scold them: after they have succeeded they are quite content. It is only by the scolding that you have demonstrated proper parental interest. . . . It is a search for proof that you love them. If you love them in the ordinary sense, the ego of such a patient is incapable of recognizing it. The path to object relationship is via sadism.

Sidney Tarachow, 1963
p. 280

ⴅ

THE MASOCHIST can be considered as someone who is struggling with a need for love, but has been saddled with a perverted technique in this quest. . . . The quest for love is processed through suffering.

Sidney Tarachow, 1963
p. 277

ⴅ

THE MASOCHIST demands so much love, so much reassurance that his objects finally get to hate him. The masochist finally creates the very situation he fears. . . . One of the difficult things to do in the treatment of a masochist is to get him to see how *much* he is really asking for, how greedy he is. He suffers from a kind of hypocritical virtue. He must be made to see this. The very sensitivity to rejection which plagues the masochist is a sign of his greed. If he were not so greedy, he would not feel rejected at every turn.

Sidney Tarachow, 1963
p. 279

ⴅ

IT COST E . . . a great deal of work to bring out and recognize how much he needed to feel preferred above everybody else. To be loved, for him, meant to be first in line for handouts. He had to find out that he was chronically angry because these needs were never really gratified, and that they never could be, as long as they were pitched so high. He had to find out, too, that his guilt over his suppressed fury made him give up the ordinary rights he should have had. . . .

Norman Cameron, 1963
p. 424

PARADOXICALLY, but not unexpectedly, Miss B. . . . got what she had always wanted from her father once she no longer needed or demanded it.

Michael Basch, 1980
p. 83

TRUE, SOME patients feel that life is not worth living without their grievances and their hate or, the other way round, without receiving full compensation for all their grievances—and the hate associated with them. Any interpretation that tries to shed a new light on the grievance is felt by those patients as if the analyst was trying to devalue the grievance. Any such attempt is felt as a threat of taking away their justification for existence; they really feel that they have nothing else to live for.

Michael Balint, 1968
pp. 182–183

THE NEGATIVISTIC or dominating patient will try to use the analytic situation as a battleground, since he feels better integrated when fighting.

Mary Julian White, 1952
p. 131

IT MUST BE kept in mind that there are a good many people who are thoroughly convinced that to irritate is their only chance for maintaining contact with another human being. . . .

Erwin Singer, 1965
p. 155

O NE FREQUENTLY meets patients who cannot bear the sense that anybody is useful to them. This inability is often caused by their intense feelings of dependence, which make them feel that the slightest degree of actual need for the analyst will result in their becoming putty in his hands and that their cravings for satisfaction of dependent needs will cause them to lose any outline and definition.

Erwin Singer, 1965
p. 339

⌿

THE INSATIABLE PATIENT

A GOURMET MEAL is a gourmet meal only if one is prepared to enjoy it in a relatively conflictless manner, which means that one is not maintaining the conviction that one does not deserve it, is too greedy, is spending too much, is being exploited by the restaurant, etc. One may eat many such meals and still end up unfed.

Ray Schafer, 1983
p. 74

⌿

T HE NONNEUROTIC patient acts on what he cannot remember, not as resistance, but because the action *is* his way of "remembering" pre-verbal trauma. He "speaks" with his feet when he walks out of a session, for example. He may be saying, "The thing that hurt me most as a baby was to be left. As soon as I could walk I made up my mind to show the other person how that feels by doing it to him."

Gertrude and Rubin Blanck, 1974
pp. 208–209

⌿

T HERE ARE CERTAIN feelings which are so constructed that they seem to be beyond words and may, therefore, have been before words when first experienced. Powerful feelings are more often than not expressed by giving another person the experience of how one feels. . . . How else can a beleaguered patient know that his analyst understands than if he suffers that experience which the patient lacks the words to describe?

James Grotstein, 1981
p. 202

〓

THE LESS STRUCTURED PATIENT

ANY STRANGER will do because there is no object independent of the state of need, but only a state of need.

Gertrude and Rubin Blanck, 1974
p. 76

〓

UNCONSCIOUSLY, our analysands are living in dread; they are trying to cope in the best way they can with infantile danger situations which have been carried forward into the present. They show us that this is so by the problems they present in the analysis.

Roy Schafer, 1983
p. 294

15

Dreams

A DREAM, THEN, is a psychosis, with all the absurdities, delusions and illusions of a psychosis. A psychosis of short duration, no doubt, harmless, even entrusted with a useful function. . . .

Sigmund Freud, 1940
p. 172

IT IS DOUBTFUL whether we could go on thinking and acting like reasonable people if we did not from time to time think and act as if we were almost crazy. In our dreams we return to ways of thinking that we deserted long ago, to emotions we no longer feel while awake.

Theodor Reik, 1952
p. 36

DREAMS . . . ARE largely, if not entirely, a reliving during sleep of the unresolved emotional problems in human relationships of our entire past life. . . .

Harry Guntrip, 1971
p. 8

THE PATIENT should learn to see his dreams as a reflection of many different trends within himself, some more acceptable to his conscious views of himself than others.

Steven Levy, 1984
p. 47

⊒

IN THIS STATE of relaxed defense, representations or derivatives of unconscious, rejected infantile tendencies more easily and openly come to conscious expression than is possible in the normal waking state.

Roy Schafer, 1954
p. 84

⊒

DREAMING IS essentially a response to urgent internal promptings. These prompting are usually needs or tensions which have not been adequately discharged during the day and which have become attached to and derive their urgency from unconscious, infantile wishes and unresolved conflict. Dreaming is at the same time a protective response to the organism's wish to sleep

Roy Schafer, 1954
p. 83

⊒

MAJOR DISTINCTIONS between the dream of the normal or neurotic ego and that of the less-intact structure is that, in the latter, capacity for secondary revision is faulty and the dream of the less-structured personality may not always protect sleep; there may be motor activity, talking in one's sleep, and even waking from anxiety in the dream.

Gertrude and Rubin Blanck, 1974
p. 235

W E SEE THAT the function of the dream is to discharge the tensions of the repressed forbidden wish: if these are extreme the dream will be charged with anxiety and the sleeper may even wake up.

Richard Chessick, 1980
p. 163

WORKING WITH DREAMS

W HEN A DREAM is first presented by the patient, silence on the part of the therapist is recommended. The dream is a virgin product of the unconscious. What direction the patient will take in conscious elaboration remains to be seen. We want to be guided by the lead of the patient's awareness and resistance, and do not wish to cue the patient in, nor to direct the material. So, first we listen.

Sheldon Roth, 1987
p. 203

W E SHOULD NOT forget Freud's dictum that even where the most compelling symbol-like content occurs in the manifest dream, we should be cautious about interpreting it fully before we collect the free associations that lead to the latent dream thoughts.

Roy Schafer, 1954
p. 96

S UPPOSE THE patient tells the dream and then seems to ignore it and begins to talk of other things. Do not interrupt. Often fifteen or twenty sentences down the therapeutic road, the patient will realize that what is being said is related to the dream and will begin to connect the material. Some superficial resistance has been worked out by the patient in this manner.

Sheldon Roth, 1987
p. 203

⊐

A DREAM, PRESENTED following an intervention, confirms that the intervention is correct in content and timing.

Gertrude and Rubin Blanck, 1974
p. 321

⊐

O FTEN, IN THE course of free association, a forgotten dream is remembered in the context of the associations and this is always more pertinent to the therapy than an artificially "remembered" dream — i.e., one that is written down. . . .

Gertrude and Rubin Blanck, 1974
p. 240

⊐

. . . E VERY WISHFUL impulse which creates a dream to-day will reappear in other dreams as long as it has not been understood and withdrawn from the domination of the unconscious. It often happens, therefore, that the best way to complete the interpretation of a dream is to leave it and to devote one's attention to a new dream, which may contain the same material in a possibly more accessible form.

Sigmund Freud, 1911
p. 94

16

Ego
Defenses

O~NE CANNOT~ flee from oneself. . . . No flight avails against danger from within; hence the ego's defence mechanisms are condemned to falsify the inner perception. . . . Not infrequently it turns out that the ego has paid too high a price for the services which these mechanisms render.

Sigmund Freud, 1937
pp. 391–392

ㄹ

T~HE MORE COMPLEX~ the behavior in question, the more desirable it is to speak of it as having a defensive aspect, rather than to call it a defense. Simply to call it a defense is to ignore its psychological intricacy.

Roy Schafer, 1954
p. 47

ㄹ

C~LINICIANS RECOGNIZE~ that the human condition makes use of all defense mechanisms at some time or other. It is the predominant use of a cluster of defenses which distinguishes one personality organization from another.

Peter Giovacchini, 1979
p. 468

⊐

PATIENTS ARE always consistent. Do not expect patients to behave differently tomorrow than they do today unless the treatment has effected some change. Everyone behaves according to his own pattern: every patient has his own favorite and typical defensive structure. Once you grasp the patient's chief line of defense, then you have a key to his dreams, to his behavior, and to his symptoms, to all his chief actions. You have the patient's style. Patients do not use many different defenses. . . . Look for the chronic pattern.

Sidney Tarachow, 1963
p. 252

⊒

REPRESSIONS

IT APPEARS ... THAT life offers little happiness to all too may adults; hence they may maintain the religious concept of future happiness in the hereafter, or they cling to the myth of past happiness in their childhood. In order to do the latter effectively, solid processes of dissociation or repression have to be activated. It requires the help of another person, the psychiatrist, who, in his turn, has come to grips with his own childhood memories, to bring them to recall.

Frieda Fromm-Reichmann, 1950
p. 55

⊒

ANY ACT OF repression cuts off a part of the personality from growth toward maturity. The successive modifications and redefinitions of impulse derivatives that normally take place during latency, adolescence, early adulthood and maturity cannot occur. Being cut off thus from ego-regulated participation in life experiences, the repressed retains its original infantile character. . . . Indeed, highly repressed adult personalities typically present a child-like appearance, some glaringly, others subtly.

Roy Schafer, 1954
p. 194

🔲

IT IS FREQUENTLY not the actual events and happenings in the previous lives of patients to which they have become oblivious but rather the emotional reactions accompanying these events or engendered by them.

Frieda Fromm-Reichmann, 1950
p. 80

🔲

ONE CAN GET in the habit of not thinking as a defense, of not perceiving and not considering what are his perceptions and feelings about life, in order to avoid what is painful.

Elvin Semrad, 1980
p. 71

🔲

DENIAL

THE METHOD . . . is based on the fantasy of the reversal of the real facts into their opposite, and is employed in situations in which it is impossible to escape some painful external impression. When a child is somewhat older, his greater freedom of physical movement and his increased powers of psychic activity enable his ego to evade such stimuli and there is no need for him to perform so complicated a psychic operation as that of denial.

Anna Freud, 1966
p. 93

THE BASIC FORMULA for denial is simple: there is no pain, no anticipation of pain, no danger. As applied to the past, the formula is; it did not happen that painful way at all. . . . It is most prominent during the early years of life before the ego and superego are fully formed and at a time when adults encourage the child's use of denial in their play with and manipulation of him. In normal development, as the highly prized ego function of reality testing is established, as real ability to avoid or transform painful external situations develops through maturation and learning, and as defenses characteristic of later stages of development crystallize, the archaic defense of denial is necessarily more or less abandoned.

Roy Schafer, 1954
p. 231

己

. . . ITS OPERATION is likely in general to be in inverse ratio to one's level of emotional maturity. It is in opposition to the vital ego function of perception and memory. Accordingly, we might suspect, and correctly so, that denial becomes less available as a psychic defense as the ego develops . . . The operation of denial may further indicate both the pervasiveness of the psychopathology which is present, and the desperateness of the internal psychologic need which calls forth such a basic and ofttimes irrational type of defensive operation.

H. P. Laughlin, 1979
pp. 57–58

己

TO THE DEGREE to which an individual must constantly guard against the development of potentially threatening inner states, to that extent is he forced to exclude perception of outer stimuli in order to prevent them from triggering recognition of his inner tendencies.

Erwin Singer, 1965
p. 176

W HEN WE FIND denial, we know that it is a reaction to external danger; when repression takes place, the ego is struggling with instinctual stimuli.

Anna Freud, 1966
p. 109

⊒

A SPECIFIC TYPE of denial commonly found is the introductory or parenthetical statement, such as "To tell the truth," "My real feelings are . . . ," "Let me be frank with you." These apparently innocuous assurances are purposeful. The patient has something to hide, and is denying it.

Roger Mackinnon and Robert Michels, 1971
p. 104

⊒

A REPUDIATED hostile impulse . . . if handled defensively and if the defense is successful, will not be felt internally and will be blocked from discharge; a state of unconscious, pent-up hostility will result.

Roy Schafer, 1954
p. 164

⊒

REACTION FORMATION

R EACTION FORMATIONS commonly take pseudo-sublimated, socially high valued forms such as generosity, tenderness, sincerity, orderliness, conscientiousness, meticulousness, manliness or femininity, bravery and altruism. The social rewards won by these reaction formations inevitably increase the tenacity with which people cling to them. . . . This consideration also helps account for the intractability of obsessive-compulsive neurotics in therapy, reaction formation being a major aspect of their defensive strategy. In the patient's eyes, the therapist seeking to bring to consciousness the impulse repudiated by the reaction formation becomes the devil's advocate.

Roy Schafer, 1954
p. 347

ㄹ

IDENTIFICATION WITH THE AGGRESSOR

So you became, in your play, like your mother, and did to your toys what she did to you.

Steven Levy, 1984
p. 105

ㄹ

Freud observed that "Identification is a substitute for a lost human relationship," or indeed for one that was urgently needed and unobtainable. Thus a child who finds that he cannot get any satisfactory kind of relationship with a parent who is too cold and aloof, or too aggressive, or too authoritarian tends to make up for his sense of apartness and isolation by identifying with, or growing like, that parent, as if this were a way of possessing the needed person within oneself.

Harry Guntrip, 1971
p. 10

ㄹ

INTROJECTION AND IDEALIZATION

These are the two most frequently used defence mechanisms in any partnership in which an oppressed, weak partner has to cope with an overwhelmingly powerful one.

Michael Balint, 1968
p. 107

PROJECTION

T HE EXTERNALIZATION of (internal) danger situations is one of the ego's earliest methods of defense against anxiety, and plays an important role in psychologic development. What happens is that the child projects his own impulses on to his objects. . . . The infant expects in fantasy that his objects (significant adults) will do to him what he has done, or that which he fantasies he has done or might wish to do, to them.

H. P. Laughlin, 1979
p. 223

⊒

. . . FEAR OF THE analyst is ultimately derived from projected hostility.

Ralph Greenson, 1967
p. 237

⊒

PROJECTIVE IDENTIFICATION

P ROJECTIVE IDENTIFICATION . . . is a psychological process that is simultaneously a type of defence, a mode of communication, a primitive form of object relationship, and a pathway for psychological change. As a defence, projective identification serves to create a sense of psychological distance from unwanted (often frightening) aspects of the self; as a mode of communication, projective identification is a process by which feelings congruent with one's own are induced in another person, thereby creating a sense of being understood by or of being "at one with" the other person. As a type of object relationship, projective identification constitutes a way of being with and relating to a partially separate object; and finally, as a pathway for psychological change, projective identification is a process by which feelings like those that one is struggling with, are psychologically processed by another person and made available for reinternalization in an altered form.

Thomas Ogden, 1979
p. 362

... THERE IS A pressure exerted by the projector on the recipient of the projection to experience himself and behave in a way congruent with the projective fantasy. This is not an imaginary pressure. This is real pressure exerted by means of a multitude of interactions between the projector and the recipient. Projective identification does not exist where there is no interaction between projector and object. . . . The "influence" is real, but it is not the imagined absolute control by means of transplanted aspects of the self inhabiting the object; rather, it is an external pressure exerted by means of interpersonal interaction.

Thomas Ogden, 1979
pp. 359–360

ꜳ

PROJECTIVE IDENTIFICATION is typically manifest as intense distrust and fear of the therapist, who is experienced as attacking the patient, while the patient himself feels empathy with the projected intense aggression and tries to control the therapist in a sadistic, overpowering way. . . . The patient's aggressive behavior, at the same time, tends to provoke from the therapist counteraggressive feelings and attitudes. . . . The danger in this situation is that under the influence of the expression of intense aggression by the patient, the reality aspects of the transference-countertransference situation may be such that it comes dangerously close to reconstituting the originally projected interaction between internalized self- and object-images.

Otto Kernberg, 1975
pp. 80–81

ꜳ

SPLITTING

WHAT ORIGINALLY was a lack of integrative capacity is gradually, in the presence of overwhelming anxiety, used defensively by the emerging ego and maintains introjections with different valences dissociated or split from each other. This serves the purpose of preventing the anxiety arising at the foci of negative introjections from being generalized throughout the ego and protects the integration of positive introjections into a primitive ego core.

Otto Kernberg, 1976
p. 36

己

THIS SPLITTING OF the object in the struggle to cope with unhappy real life experience leads to a splitting of the ego in the struggle to maintain relations with both good and bad aspects of the mother and other family figures.

Harry Guntrip, 1971
p. 98

己

IT IS GEARED to protect the ideal, good relationship with mother from "contamination" by bad self-representations and bad representations of her.

Otto Kernberg, 1976
p. 67

己

REGRESSION

THE CONCEPT OF regression is often misunderstood. It does not mean a return to infancy or childhood, or even a general reversion to behavior that is normal for an infant or a child. Adults are organized in ways that infants and children are not. When they regress, they reactivate infantile conflicts, wishes and fears, but most of their adult defensive and coping organization remains. The regressed adult does not act, speak or look like a child.

Norman Cameron, 1963
p. 121

THROUGH THE automatic and consciously effortless process . . . the ego retreats toward a safer and more defensible position, toward the only ones it knows — those already experienced, a more satisfactory era from the past. Such a retreat reflects an inability to cope with life as it is experienced, some significant aspect of living, or the current situation.

H. P. Laughlin, 1979
p. 320

THE MORE PROFOUND the patient's pathology, the more far-reaching his abandoning growth, vision, and awareness, the more pervasive his deeply ingrained belief system about the nature of his fellow men, what they will tolerate and what they will condemn, under what circumstances they will let him live and what will occasion their wrath and anxiety-provoking behavior.

Erwin Singer, 1965
p. 264

THE ADULT EGO with its greater strength continues to defend itself against dangers which no longer exist in reality and even finds itself impelled to seek out those real situations which may serve as a substitute for the original danger, so as to be able to justify its clinging to its habitual modes of reaction.

Sigmund Freud, 1937
p. 392

UNCONSCIOUSLY, we repeatedly enact infantile dangers and security measures.

Roy Schafer, 1983
p. 46

REFERENCES

Alexander, F. (1925). Review of *The Development of Psychoanalysis* by S. Ferenczi and O. Rank. *International Journal of Psychoanalysis* 6:484-496.

_____ (1935). The problem of psychoanalytic technique. *Psychoanalytic Quarterly* 4:588-611.

_____ (1946). The principle of flexibility. In *Psychoanalytic Therapy: Principles and Application* , ed. F. Alexander and T. French, pp. 25-65. New York: Ronald Press.

Arieti, S. (1974).*Interpretation of Schizophrenia*. New York: Basic Books.

Arlow, J. (1980). The genesis of interpretation. In *Psychoanalytic Explorations of Technique*, ed. H. Blum, pp. 139-206. New York: International Universities Press.

Balint, M (1968). *The Basic Fault: Therapeutic Aspects of Regression*. New York: Brunner/Mazel.

Bauer, G., and Kobos, J. (1987). *Brief Therapy: Short-Term Psychodynamic Intervention*. Northvale, NJ: Jason Aronson.

Basch, M. (1980). *Doing Psychotherapy*. New York: Basic Books.

_____ (1985). Interpretation: toward a developmental model. In *Progress in Self Psychology*, vol. 1, ed. A. Goldberg, pp. 33-42. New York: Guilford Press.

Beier, E. (1966).*The Silent Language of Psychotherapy*. Chicago: Aldine.

Bellak, L. (1980). Brief and emergency psychotherapy. In *Specialized Techniques in Individual Psychotherapy*, ed. T. Karasu and L. Bellak, pp. 45-75. New York: Brunner/Mazel.

Bellak, L.,and Faithorn, P. (1981).*Crises and Special Problems in Psychoanalysis and Psychotherapy*. New York: Brunner/Mazel.

Bemporad, J. (1980). Review of *Object Relations Theory in the Light of Cognitive Development*. *Journal of the American Academy of Psychoanalysis* 8:57-75.

Bion, W. (1967). Notes on memory and desire. *The Psychoanalytic Forum* 2:271-281.

Blanck, G., and Blanck, R. (1974). *Ego Psychology Theory and Practice.* New York: Columbia University Press.

———— (1979). *Ego Psychology II.* New York: Columbia University Press.

Brenner, C. (1979). Working alliance, therapeutic alliance and transference. *Journal of the American Psychoanalytic Association* 27:137–157.

Breuer, J., and Freud, S. (1895). Studies on hysteria. *Standard Edition* 2:1–310.

Bromberg, P. (1984). The third ear. In *Clinical Perspectives on the Supervision of Psychoanalysis and Psychotherapy*, ed. L. Caligor, P. Bromberg, and J. Meltzer, pp. 29–44. New York: Plenum.

Bruner, J. (1957). Freud and the images of man. In *Freud and the 20th Century*, ed. B. Nelson. New York: Meridian Books.

Caligor, L. (1981). Parallel and reciprocal processes in psychoanalytic supervision. *Contemporary Psychoanalysis* 17:1–27.

Cameron, N. (1963). *Personality Development and Psychopathology—A Dynamic Approach.* Boston: Houghton Mifflin.

Chessick, R. (1974). *Technique and Practice of Intensive Psychotherapy.* New York: Jason Aronson.

———— (1979). A practical approach to the psychotherapy of the borderline patient. *American Journal of Psychotherapy* 33:531–536.

———— (1980). *Freud Teaches Psychotherapy.* Indianapolis: Hackett Publishing.

———— (1985). *Psychology of the Self and the Treatment of Narcissism.* Northvale, NJ: Jason Aronson.

Colby, K. (1958). *A Skeptical Psychoanalyst.* New York: Ronald Press.

Cooper, A.,and Witenberg, E. (1983). Stimulation of curiosity in the supervisory process. *Contemporary Psychoanalysis* 19:248–264.

Crowley, R. (1977). Sullivan's concept of participant-observation (a symposium). *Contemporary Psychoanalysis* 13:347–386.

———— (1984). Being and doing in continuous consultation for psychoanalytic education. In *Clinical Perspectives on the Supervision of Psychoanalysis and Psychotherapy*, ed. L. Caligor, P. Bromberg, and J. Meltzer, pp. 75–88. New York: Plenum.

Davanloo, H. (1980). A method of short-term dynamic psychotherapy. In *Short-Term Dynamic Psychotherapy*, ed. H. Davanloo, pp. 43–74. Northvale, NJ: Jason Aronson.

Debell, D. (1981). Supervisory styles and positions. In *Becoming a Psychoanalyst*, ed. R. Wallerstein pp. 39–60. New York: International Universities Press.

Dewald, P. (1964). *Psychotherapy: A Dynamic Approach.* New York: Basic Books.

———— (1976). Toward a general concept of the therapeutic process. *International Journal of Psychoanalytic Psychotherapy* 5:283–299.

Dorpat, T. (1977). On neutrality. *International Journal of Psychoanalytic Psychotherapy* 6:39–64.

Druck, A. (1989). *Four Therapeutic Approaches to the Borderline Patient.* Northvale, NJ: Jason Aronson.

Eisenstein S. (1980). The contributions of Franz Alexander. In *Short-Term Psychodynamic Psychotherapy*, ed. H. Davanloo, pp. 25–42. New York: Jason Aronson.

Eissler, K. (1953). The effect of the structure of the ego on psychoanalytic technique. *Journal of the American Psychoanalytic Association* 1:104–143.

Epstein, L. (1979). The therapeutic use of countertransference data with borderline patients. *Contemporary Psychoanalysis* 15:248–275.

_____ (1982). Adapting to the patient's therapeutic need in the psychoanalytic situation. *Contemporary Psychoanalysis* 18:190–217.

Epstein, L., and Feiner, A. (1979). Countertransference: the therapist's contribution to treatment. *Contemporary Psychoanalysis* 15:489–513.

Farberow, N., Helig, S., and Litman, R. (1970). Evaluation and management of suicidal persons. In *The Psychology of Suicide*, ed. E. Shneidman, N. Farberow, and R. Litman, pp. 273–292. Northvale, NJ: Jason Aronson.

Fenichel, O. (1941). *Problems of Psychoanalytic Technique*. New York: Psychoanalytic Quarterly.

_____ (1945). *The Psychoanalytic Theory of Neurosis*. New York: Norton.

Ferenczi, S. (1921). The further development of an active therapy in psychoanalysis. In *Further Contributions to the Theory and Technique of Psychoanalysis*, ed. J. Rickman, pp. 198–217. London: Hogarth Press, 1950.

_____ (1928). The elasticity of psychoanalytic technique. In *Final Contributions to the Problems and Methods of Psychoanalysis*, ed. M. Balint, pp. 87–101. London: Hogarth Press, 1955.

Fine, R. (1979). *The Intimate Hour*. Wayne, NJ: Avery Publishing Group.

Flegenheimer, W. (1982). *Techniques of Brief Psychotherapy*. New York: Jason Aronson.

Fliess, R. (1942). The metapsychology of the analyst. *Psychoanalytic Quarterly* 11:211–227.

French, T. (1946). The dynamics of the therapeutic process. In *Psychoanalytic Therapy Principles and Application*, ed. F. Alexander and T. French, pp.132–144. New York: Ronald Press.

Freud, A. (1966). *The Ego and the Mechanisms of Defense* (Revised Edition). New York: International Universities Press.

_____ (1980). Insight and self-observation. In *The Technique of Child Psychoanalysis Discussions with Anna Freud*, ed. J. Sandeler, H. Kennedy, and R. Tyson, pp. 67–73. Cambridge, MA: Harvard University Press.

Freud, S. (1895). Psychotherapy of hysteria. *Standard Edition* 2:1–310.

_____ (1905a). Fragment of an analysis of a case of hysteria. *Standard Edition* 7:7–122.

_____ (1905b). On psychotherapy. *Standard Edition* 4:257–268.

_____ (1910). Observations on wild psychoanalysis. *Standard Edition* 11:219–227.

_____ (1911). The handling of dream interpretation in psychoanalysis. *Standard Edition* 12:89–96.

_____ (1912a). The dynamics of transference. *Standard Edition* 12:99–108.

_____ (1912b). Recommendations to physicians practicing psychoanalysis. *Standard Edition* 12:111–120.

_____ (1913). On beginning the treatment. *Standard Edition* 12:123–144.

_____ (1914). Remembering, repeating and working through. *Standard Edition* 12:145–157.

_____ (1915). Observations on transference love. *Standard Edition* 12:157–172.

_____ (1919). Lines of advance in psychoanalytic therapy. *Standard Edition* 17:157–168.

_____ (1920). Beyond the pleasure principle. *Standard Edition* 18:7–64.

_____ (1926). The question of lay analysis. *Standard Edition* 20:179–258.

_____ (1937). Analysis terminable and interminable.*International Journal of Psycho-Analysis* 18:373–405.

_____ (1940). An outline of psychoanalysis. *Standard Edition* 23:139–207.

Friedman, L. (1978). Trends in the psychoanalytic theory of treatment.*Psychoanalytic Quarterly* 47:524-567.

Fromm-Reichmann, F. (1950). *Principles of Intensive Psychotherapy*. Chicago: University of Chicago Press.

Gerber, L. (1974/1975). Countertransference with a hostile-dependent patient: what the books don't tell you. *Voices* 10:56–60.

Gill, M. (1979). The analysis of the transference. *Journal of American Psychoanalytic Association* 27:263–288.

_____ (1982). *The Analysis of Transference*, vol. 1. New York: International Universities Press.

Giovacchini, P. (1979). *Treatment of Primitive Mental States*. New York: Jason Aronson.

_____ (1982). *A Clinician's Guide to Reading Freud*. New York: Jason Aronson.

Glover, E. (1955). *The Technique of Psychoanalysis*. New York: International Universities Press.

Goldberg, A. (1985). The definition and role of interpretation. In *Progress in Self Psychology*, vol. 1, ed. A. Goldberg, pp. 62–68. New York: Guilford Press.

Greenacre, P. (1954). The role of transference. *Journal of the American Psychoanalytic Association* 2:671–684.

Greenson, R. (1960). Empathy and its vicissitudes. *International Journal of Psycho-Analysis* 41:418–424.

_____ (1967). *The Technique and Practice of Psychoanalysis*. New York: International Universities Press.

Grotstein, J. (1981). *Splitting and Projective Identification*. New York: Jason Aronson.

Guntrip, H. (1969). *Schzoid Phenomena Object-Relations and the Self*. New York: International Universities Press.

_____ (1971). *Psychoanalytic Theory, Therapy, and the Self*. New York: Basic Books.

_____ (1975). My experience of analysis with Fairbairn and Winnicott. *International Review of Psychoanalysis*. 2:145–156.

Gustafson, J. (1986). *The Complex Secret of Brief Psychotherapy*. New York: Norton.

Guthiel, E. (1959). Problems of therapy in obsessive-compulsive neurosis.*American Journal of Psychotherapy* 13:793–808.

Hartmann, H. (1951). Technical implication of ego psychology. *Psychoanalytic Quarterly* 20:31–43.

Heimann, P. (1950). On countertransference. *International Journal of Psycho-Analysis* 31:81–84.

Horner, A. (1980). Object relations, the self and the therapeutic matrix. *Contemporary Psychoanalysis* 16:186–203.

_____ (1985). The Oedipus complex. In *Treating the Oedipal Patient in Brief Psychotherapy*, ed. A. Horner, pp. 25–54. Northvale, NJ: Jason Aronson.

Hunt, W., and Issacharoff, A. (1977). Heinrich Racker and countertransference

Theory. *Journal of the American Academy of Psychoanalysis* 5:95–105.

Jung, C. G. (1933). *Modern Man in Search of a Soul.* New York: Harvest Books.

———— (1961). *Memories, Dreams, Reflections.* New York: Pantheon.

Kernberg, O. (1965). Notes on countertransference. *Journal of the American Psychoanalytic Association* 13:38–56.

———— (1975). *Borderline Conditions and Pathological Narcissism.* New York: Jason Aronson.

———— (1976).*Object-Relations Theory and Clinical Psychoanalysis.* New York: Jason Aronson.

———— (1977). The structural diagnosis of the borderline personality organization. In *Borderline Personality Disorder: The Concept, the Syndrome, the Patient,* ed. P. Hartocellis, pp. 87–122. New York: International Universities Press.

———— (1982). The theory of psychoanalytic psychotherapy. In *Curative Factors in Dynamic Psychotherapy,* ed. S. Slipp, pp. 21–43. New York: McGraw-Hill.

———— (1984). *Severe Personality Disorders.* New Haven, CT: Yale University Press.

Khan, M. (1969). Vicissitudes of being, knowing and experiencing in the therapeutic situation. *British Journal of Medical Psychology* 42:383–393.

Kohut, H. (1971). *The Analysis of the Self.* New York: International Universities Press.

———— (1977). *The Restoration of the Self.* New York: International Universities Press.

Kroll, J. (1988). *The Challenge of the Borderline Patient.* New York: Norton.

Kubie, L. (1971). The destructive potential of humor in psychotherapy. *American Journal of Psychiatry* 127:861–866.

Langs, R. (1975). The therapeutic relationship and deviations in technique.*International Journal of Psychoanalytic Psychotherapy* 4:106–141.

———— (1976). *The Bipersonal Field.* New York: Jason Aronson.

Laughlin, H. P. (1979). *The Ego and Its Defenses.* New York: Jason Aronson.

Lesser, R. (1984). Supervision: illusions, anxieties, and questions. In *Clinical Perspectives on the Supervision of Psychoanalysis and Psychotherapy,* ed. L. Caligor, P. Bromberg, and J. Meltzer, pp. 143–152. New York: Plenum.

Levenson, E. (1982). Follow the fox. *Contemporary Psychoanalysis* 18:1–15.

Levy, S. (1984). *Principles of Interpretation.* New York: Jason Aronson.

Lindner, R. (1982). *The Fifty-Minute Hour: A Collection of True Psychoanalytic Tales.* New York: Jason Aronson.

Litman, R. (1970a). Suicide as acting out. In *The Psychology of Suicide,* ed. E. Shneidman, N. Farberow, and R. Litman, pp. 293–306. New York: Jason Aronson.

———— (1970b). Treatment of the potentially suicidal patient. In *The Psychology of Suicide,* ed. E. Shneidman, N. Farberow, and R. Litman, pp. 405–414. New York: Jason Aronson.

Litman, R., and Farberow, N. (1970). Emergency evaluation of suicidal potential. In *The Psychology of Suicide,* ed. E. Shneidman, N. Farberow, and R. Litman, pp. 259–272. New York: Jason Aronson.

Mackinnon, R., and Michels, R. (1971). *The Psychiatric Interview in Clinical Practice.* Philadelphia: W. B. Saunders.

Malan, D. (1979). *Individual Psychotherapy and the Science of Psychodynamics.* London: Butterworths.

Malcolm, J. (1981). *Psychoanalysis: The Impossible Profession.* New York: Knopf.

Marmor, J. (1979a). Change in psychoanalytic treatment. *Journal of The American Academy of Psychoanalysis* 7:345–357.

———— (1979b). Short-term dynamic psychotherapy. *American Journal of Psychiatry* 136:149–153.

Masterson, J. C. (1976). *Psychotherapy of the Borderline Adult.* New York: Brunner/Mazel.

———— (1983). *Countertransference and Psychotherapeutic Technique/Teaching Seminars on Psychotherapy of the Borderline Adult.* New York: Brunner/Mazel.

Menninger, K. (1958). *Theory of Psychoanalytic Technique.* New York: Basic Books.

Mueller, W., and Aniskiewicz. A. (1986). *Psychotherapeutic Intervention in Hysterical Disorders.* New York: Jason Aronson.

Nemiah, J. C. (1973). *Foundations of Psychopathology.* New York: Jason Aronson.

Ogden, T. (1979). On projective identification. *International Journal of Psycho-Analysis* 60:357–373.

Ornstein. P., and Ornstein, A. (1985). Clinical understanding and explaining: the empathic vantage point. In *Progress in Self Psychology*, vol. 1, ed. A. Goldberg, pp. 43–61. New York: Guilford Press.

Paolino, T. (1981). *Psychoanalytic Psychotherapy: Theory, Technique, Therapeutic Relationship and Treatability.* New York: Brunner/Mazel.

Paul, I. (1978). *The Form and Technique of Psychotherapy.* Chicago: University of Chicago Press.

Reich, W. (1949). *Character Analysis* (3rd ed.). New York: The Noonday Press.

Reik, T. (1952). *Listening with the Third Ear.* New York: Farrar, Straus.

Roskin, G., and Rabiner, C. (1976). Psychotherapists' passivity—a major training problem. *International Journal of Psychoanalytic Psychotherapy* 5:319–331.

Roth, S. (1970). The seemingly ubiquitous depression following acute schizophrenic episodes. *American Journal of Psychiatry* 127:51–58.

———— (1987).*Psychotherapy: The Art of Wooing Nature.* Northvale, NJ: Jason Aronson.

Rycroft, C. (1966). *Psychoanalysis Observed.* London: Constable.

Salzman, L. (1980). *Treatment of the Obsessive Personality.* New York: Jason Aronson.

Sandler, J. (1976). Countertransference and role-responsiveness. *International Review of Psychoanalysis* 3:43–47.

Sandler, J., Holder, A., Kawenoka, M., et al. (1969). Notes on some theoretical and clinical aspects of transference. *International Journal of Psycho-Analysis* 50:633–645.

Saul, L. (1967). Goals of psychoanalytic psychotherapy. In *The Goals of Psychotherapy*, ed. A. Mahrer, pp. 41–58. East Norwalk, CT: Appleton Century Crofts.

Schact, T., Binder, J., and Strupp, H. (1984). The dynamic focus. In *Psychotherapy in a New Key—A Guide to Time—Limited Psychotherapy*, ed. H. Strupp and J. Binder, pp. 65–109. New York: Basic Books.

Schafer, F. (1954). *Psychoanalytic Interpretation in Rorschach Testing.* New York: Grune & Stratton.

Schafer, R. (1983). *The Analytic Attitude.* New York: Basic Books.

Seinfeld, J. (1990). *The Bad Object, Handling the Negative Therapeutic Reaction in Psychotherapy.* Northvale, NJ: Jason Aronson.

Semrad, E. (1980). *Semrad, The Heart of a Therapist,* ed. S. Rako and H. Mazer. New York: Jason Aronson.

Sharpe, E. (1930). The technique of psychoanalysis. In *Collected Papers on Psychoanalysis,* ed. M. Brierly. London: Hogarth Press, 1950.

Sifneos, P. (1980). Motivation for change. In *Short-term Psychodynamic Psychotherapy,* ed. H. Davanloo, pp. 93–98. New York: Jason Aronson.

Singer, E. (1965). *Key Concepts in Psychotherapy.* New York: Basic Books.

Spotnitz, H. (1976). *Psychotherapy of Preoedipal Conditions.* New York: Jason Aronson.

Strachey, J. (1934). The nature of the therapeutic action of psychoanalysis. *International Journal of Psycho-Analysis* 15:127–159.

Strachey, J. (1937). Therapeutic results of psychoanalysis. *International Journal of Psycho-Analysis* 18:139–145.

Stone, L. (1961). *The Psychoanalytic Situation.* New York: International Universities Press.

Strupp, H. (1977). A reformulation of the dynamics of the therapist's contribution. In *Effective Psychotherapy: A Handbook of Research,* ed. A. Gurman and A. Razin, pp. 3–21. New York: Pergamon Press.

Strupp, H., and Binder, J. (1984). *Psychotherapy in a New Key — A Guide to Time-limited Psychotherapy.* New York: Basic Books.

Sullivan, H. S. (1947). *Conceptions Of Modern Psychiatry.* New York: Norton.

——— (1954). *The Psychiatric Interview.* New York: Norton.

Szasz, T. (1963). The concept of transference. *International Journal of Psycho-Analysis* 44:432–443 .

Tarachow, S. (1963). *An Introduction to Psychotherapy.* New York: International Universities Press.

Thompson, C. (1952). Sullivan and psychoanalysis. In *The Contributions of Harry Stack Sullivan,* ed. P. Mullahy, pp. 101–115. New York: Science House.

——— (1964). Countertransference. In *Interpersonal Psychoanalysis — The Selected Papers of Clara Thompson,* ed. M. Green, pp. 162–167. New York: Basic Books.

Valiant, G. (1977). *Adaptation to Life.* Boston: Little Brown.

White, M. (1952). Sullivan and treatment. In *The Contributions of Harry Stack Sullivan,* ed. P. Mullahy, pp. 117–150. New York: Science House.

Wile, D. (1972). Negative countertransference and therapist discouragement. *International Journal of Psychoanalytic Psychotherapy* 1:36–67.

Winnicott, D. W. (1949). Hate in the countertransference. *International Journal of Psycho-Analysis* 30:69–74.

——— (1953). Transitional objects and transitional phenomena. *International Journal of Psycho-Analysis* 34:89–97.

——— (1955). Metapsychological and clinical aspects of regression within the psychoanalytic set-up. *International Journal of Psycho-Analysis* 36:16–26.

Yalom, I. (1980). *Existential Psychotherapy.* New York: Basic Books.

Credits

The editor gratefully acknowledges the following publishers and journals for their generous permission to use quotations from copyrighted works:

From *Sigmund Freud: Collected Papers*, Volume II. Authorized Translation under the supervision of Joan Riviere. Published by arrangement with The Hogarth Press, Ltd., and the Institute of Psycho-Analysis, London. Reprinted by permission of Basic Books, Inc., Publishers, New York.

From *Sigmund Freud: Collected Papers*, Volume III. Authorized Translation by Alix and James Strachey. Published by arrangement with The Hogarth Press, Ltd., and the Institute of Psycho-Analysis, London. Reprinted by permission of Basic Books, Inc., Publishers, New York.

From *Psychoanalytic Theory, Therapy and the Self* by Harry J. S. Guntrip. © 1971 by Basic Books, Inc. Reprinted by permission of Basic Books, Inc., Publishers, New York.

From *Final Contributions to the Problems and Methods of Psychoanalysis* by Sandor Ferenczi, ed. Michael Balint. © 1955 by Basic Books, Inc.

From Michael Balint, *The Basic Fault: Therapeutic Aspects of Regression.* © 1968. Reprinted by permission of Tavistock Publications.

From *The Psychiatric Interview in Clinical Practice* by Roger Mckinnon, M.D., and Robert Michels, M.D. Copyright © 1971 by W. B. Saunders Co. Reprinted by permission of the authors.

Reprinted from *The Psychoanalytic Theory of Neurosis* by Otto Fenichel, M.D., by permission of W. W. Norton & Company, Inc. Copyright 1945 by W. W. Norton & Company, Inc. Copyright renewed 1972 by Hana Fenichel.

Index

297

Semrad, E.
  on ego defenses, 277
  on exploratory versus supportive
      therapy, 221
  on feelings, 82, 83
  on identification/character
      formation, 246, 248, 250
  on positive transference, 120
  on style of interpretation, 166
  on symptom cures, 112
  on therapeutic goals, 91
  on treatment of prepsychotic
      panic/active decompensation, 60
  on use of hospital, 212
Sharpe, E. F.
  on negative therapeutic reaction, 154
  on psychodynamics, 255
  on therapeutic goals, 86
Sifneos, P.
  on motivation, 48
Singer, E.
  on advances in understanding
      transference, 135, 137
  on aggression, 267, 268
  on analyst setting termination date,
      117
  on change, in psychotherapy, 108
  on countertransference, 179
  on denial, 278
  on erotic component in positive
      transference, 144
  on exploratory versus supportive
      therapy, 220
  on evenly suspended attention, 5
  on hostility of patient toward
      therapist, 182
  on initial interview, 37
  on negative therapeutic reaction, 151,
      152
  on neutrality, 12
  on psychodynamics, 255
  on regression, 284
  on reliability of therapist, 200
  on silence, at beginning of hour, 19
  on symptom cures, 109–110
  on termination, 113

  on therapeutic ambition, 99
  on therapeutic goals, 87
  on working through, 75
Spotnitz, H.
  on use of hospital, 213
Stone, L.
  on anonymity, 34
  on patient–therapist attachment, 127
Strachey, J.
  on change, in psychotherapy, 108
  on early interpretations, 174, 175
  on transference, 132
Strupp, H.
  on advances in understanding
      transference, 135, 136, 137, 139
  on analyst setting termination date,
      115
  on change, in psychotherapy, 109
  on development of focus, 103
  on diagnosis, 43
  on early interpretations, 171
  on negative therapeutic reaction, 155
  on positive transference, 121
  on resistance to transference, 134
  on respect, 21, 23, 25
  on symptom cures, 111
  on therapeutic goals, 90
  on time limit for therapy, 105
  on use of questions, 42
  on working through, 71, 72–73, 76,
      77
Sullivan, H. S.
  on early interpretations, 170–171
  on identification/character
      formation, 251
  on initial interview, 37–38
  on interpretation, 163
  on interviewing style, 38, 39
  on reliability of therapist, 201
  on repetition compulsion, 260
  on supervision, 232–233
  on therapeutic goals, 87–88, 89, 90–91
  on therapy for therapists, 234–235
  on treatment of decompensated
      patients, 214–215
  on use of questions, 42